JUDAISM IN THE
MATRIX OF
CHRISTIANITY

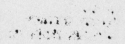

JUDAISM IN THE MATRIX OF CHRISTIANITY

Jacob Neusner

FORTRESS PRESS   PHILADELPHIA

140024

Library of Congress Cataloging-in-Publication Data

Neusner, Jacob, 1932–
    Judaism in the matrix of Christianity.

    Includes index.
    1. Rabbinical literature—History and criticism.
    2. Judaism—Relations—Christianity. 3. Christianity
and other religions—Judaism. 4. Bible. O.T.—
Criticism, interpretation, etc., Jewish. I. Title.
    BM496.5.N48   1986   296.3′872   85–45492
    ISBN 0–8006–1897–1

1830D86   Printed in the United States of America   1–1897

For my daughter
Margalit Leah Berakhah
on the occasion of her becoming a bat mitzvah

Contents

Preface

This book completes the exposition begun in *Judaism in the Beginning of Christianity* (Philadelphia: Fortress Press, 1984). That book analyzes the way in which Christianity took shape in the matrix of Judaism. This one turns to the mirror-opposite: Judaism as it took shape in the matrix of Christianity—but a different Judaism and a different Christianity—as explained in the Introduction.

We deal with three important changes that first emerge in the writings of the sages of the Land of Israel that reached closure at the end of the fourth and the beginning of the fifth century, one a massive commentary to the Mishnah as shall be explained, and other equally impressive commentaries to books of Scripture. All these changes constitute shifts in the symbolic system and structure of the Judaism then taking shape. What I propose is not merely that things changed, but that things took the particular changes they did because of a critical challenge: the triumph of Christianity. The symbolic system of Christianity, with Christ triumphant, with the cross as the now-regnant symbol, with the canon of Christianity now defined and recognized as authoritative, called forth from the sages of the Land of Israel a symbolic system strikingly responsive to the crisis. That system focused upon the coming of the Messiah set as the teleology of the system of Judaism as they defined that system, the symbol of the Torah expanded to encompass the whole of human existence as the system laid forth the limns of that existence, the canon of Sinai broadened to take account of the entirety of the sages' teachings, as much as of the written Torah everyone acknowledged as authoritative. Did the sages say these things in order to answer the challenge of Christianity? No one can claim that they did. We cannot speculate on motive since we have no evidence by which to test our speculation. All we can do is point to the contrast between the sages' system as revealed in writings closed in the later second and third century, in particular the Mishnah and its closely allied documents, and the system that emerged in the writings of the later fourth and fifth centuries. The contrast tells the tale.

However diverse the Judaisms of the past, a single symbol stands for Judaism. That is the Torah. So the history of Judaism as we now know it must sort out its facts in the story of the Torah, its contents and meaning, and how Israel, the Jewish people, became definitively and distinctively the people of the Torah. We begin with a simple and clear definition of the Judaism predominant today and for twenty prior centuries. Judaism is the religion of the Torah, that is, of instruction of God's will revealed by God to Israel through Moses at Mount Sinai. A further detail is critical even at the outset. The definition of the Torah of Sinai encompasses more than the Pentateuch or even the entirety of the Hebrew Bible or "Old Testament." In the view of Judaism the Torah came to Moses in two media; one in writing, that is, the Scriptures, the other in the medium of memory, that is, orally. Thus Judaism is comprised of "the written Torah," and "the oral Torah." Judaism therefore is the religion of the dual Torah, and Judaists, people who believe in and practice Judaism, are those who accept and follow the religion of the "one whole Torah of Moses, our rabbi."

The simple definition of Judaism as the religion of the "one whole Torah of Moses, our rabbi" derives from the classical period in the history of Judaism. It speaks today for those who affirm the classical teachings of Judaism, whether in the Orthodox, the Reform, the Conservative, or the Reconstructionist expression of those teachings. But Judaism in the definition just given took shape over a long period of time. In fact there are three periods into which the history of Judaism is to be divided. The first was the formative age, from the period of the formation of the Hebrew Scriptures, ca. 500 B.C.E., to the closure of the Talmud of Babylonia, ca. 600 C.E. The second was the classical age from late antiquity to the nineteenth century, in which that original definition dominated the lives of the Jewish people nearly everywhere they lived. The third has been the modern age from the nineteenth century to our own day, when an essentially religious understanding of what it means to be Israel, the Jewish people, came to compete with other views and other symbolic expressions of those views. In the first period there were various Judaisms, diverse compositions of a worldview and a way of life that people believed represented God's will for Israel, the Jewish people. During that long age—nearly a thousand years from the closure of the Hebrew Scriptures to the conclusion of the principal document of Judaism, the Talmud of Babylonia (which we shall consider later on)—the Judaism of the dual Torah came into being and competed for Jews' loyalty with other Judaisms. In the second period a single Judaism predominated, the one teaching the dual Torah of Sinai. During that time the important ideas or issues developed by Jews were worked out within the categories of the Judaism of the dual Torah. For example, a variety of mystical ideas and practices entered the world of Judaism and attained naturalization within the Torah. In the third or modern period the diversity characteristic of the period of origins has again come to prevail. Now the symbolic system and structure of the Judaism of the dual Torah competes for Jews' attention with other Judaic systems on the one side, and with a wildly diverse range of symbols of other-than-Jewish origin and meaning on the other.

But what of the Judaism of the dual Torah in relationship to the life of Israel, the Jewish people over time (not to be identified only with the contemporary State of Israel which came into being in 1948)? That Judaism of the dual Torah endured and flourishes today as the religion of a small group of people. In the formulation of the sages of the Mishnah and the Talmud, books we shall presently take up, the Torah confronted the challenge of the cross of Christianity and later on the sword and crescent of Islam as well. Within Israel, the Jewish people, the Torah triumphed. If we understand how rabbinic Judaism met the crisis of Christianity in its triumphant form as ruler of the world from the time of Constantine in the fourth century, we also will grasp why Judaism as the rabbis defined it succeeded through history from that time to this. For when Christianity arose to define the civilization of the West, Judaism met and overcame its greatest crisis. It held. As a result, Jews remained within the system. They continued for the entire history of the West to conduct life in accord with the way of life of the Torah as the rabbis explained it.

To state matters simply, with the triumph of Christianity through Constantine and his successors in the West, Christianity's explicit claims, now validated in world-shaking events of the age, demanded a reply. The sages of the Talmud provided it. At those very specific points at which the Christian challenge met head-on with old Israel's worldview, the sages' doctrines responded. What did Israel's sages have to present as the Torah's answer to the cross? It was the Torah. This took three forms. The Torah was defined first in the doctrine of the Mishnah as oral and memorized revelation, and, by implication, other rabbinical writings fell into the same category of Torah. The Torah, moreover, was presented as the encompassing symbol of Israel's salvation. Finally, the Torah was embodied in the person of the Messiah who of course would be a rabbi. The Torah in all three modes confronted the cross with its doctrine of the triumphant Christ, Messiah and king, ruler now of earth as of heaven.

What was the outcome? A stunning success for the society for which the sages—and, in the sages' view, God—cared so deeply: eternal Israel after the flesh. For Judaism in the rabbis' statement did endure in the Christian West, imparting to Israel the secure conviction that it was that Israel after the flesh to which the Torah continued to speak. How do we know the sages' Judaism won? Because in turn, when Islam gained its victory, Christianity throughout the Middle East and North Africa gave way. But the sages' Judaism in those same vast territories retained the loyalty and conviction of the people of the Torah. The cross would rule only where the crescent and its sword did not. Yet the Torah of Sinai everywhere and always sanctified Israel in time and promised secure salvation for eternity. So Israel believed and so does faithful Israel, those Jews who also are Judaists, believe today. The entire history of Judaism is contained within these simple propositions.

Since this book is made up of free-standing essays, with the argument unfolding at the interstices, in closing let me state in a systematic way the fundamental case I propose to make here. My proposition is that it was in direct response to the challenge of Christianity triumphant that the Judaism of the dual Torah took shape in the fourth century, and came to its first documentary expression in the writings of the early fifth century.

Two facts demonstrate that proposition: change in some things, stability in others. That is to say, first, some important matters of symbol and doctrine changed in the fourth century; second, other critical doctrines remained the same. The character of the difference between what changed and what remained stable points toward Christianity as the generative force for the reform of the Judaic system of the Mishnah and its transformation into the Judaism of the dual Torah. Specifically, the canonical history of the formation of the principal ideas of the Judaism of the dual Torah in the documents composed at the end of the fourth century shows four important, systemically critical, points of change. The fact that these changes matter is exposed by comparison with two significant matters of doctrine and structure that do not change. So as we trace the history of ideas across the unfolding writings of the ancient sages of Judaism, we see that some ideas change, others do not. I propose here to demonstrate that fact of change in some indicative matters and stability in others and to account for the difference. Let us deal first with the facts.

First, two important components of the system of the Judaism of the dual Torah, the doctrine of emotions and the structure of sanctification, remained stable in the unfolding of the canonical documents of that Judaism. These are the propositions of chapters 2 and 3.

Second, four important components reveal striking change: the doctrines of Rome, the Messiah, and the Torah, and the composition of books of exegesis of Scripture. In the Mishnaic system Rome was a place; it became a sibling rival of Israel. In the Mishnaic system the Messiah theme served as an aspect of taxonomy. It became central to the systemic teleology of the Judaism of the dual Torah. In the Mishnaic system the Torah had served as a book and a status. It became the critical symbol of the Judaism at hand, transformed into the medium for the doctrine of salvation. Documents of exegesis of the Mishnah, organized around the layout of the Mishnah, were joined by documents containing exegesis of books of Scripture and organized around the layout of Scripture's books as the counterpart to the Mishnah's tractates, in particular Genesis, Leviticus, Numbers, and Deuteronomy. In all four instances, the writings that came to redaction, scholarship generally maintains, by the end of the fourth century[1] contain those evidences of change that we have traced. These are the facts established in chapter 5, 6, 7, and 8, and inquiry based on the method spelled out in chapter 4.

The explanation of why change affected some matters of doctrine and not others then is spelled out in chapter 1. The main point may be simply stated.

What remained stable were components of the Judaic system that dealt with enduring facts which the conversion of Constantine did not affect: political subjugation, persisting materially unaffected by the Christian emperors; stress on the ongoing sanctification of the everyday as the mode of defining who is Israel, unchanged by the shift in history marked in Christianity's rise to power. What changed were those components of the Judaism of the dual Torah—mode of symbolization of Rome, means of working out the results of the exegetical method, definition of systemic teleology and restatement in historical and eschatological terms, and central symbol of the whole—that came into question because of the political consequences of the Christianization of the Roman Empire.

---

1. The dates of Genesis Rabbah and Leviticus Rabbah at ca. 400–450 are unanimously affirmed. Those of Sifra to Leviticus, Sifre to Numbers, and Sifre to Deuteronomy, are not. Because all sayings in those writings are attributed to names that occur, also, in the Mishnah, nineteenth-century scholarship, taking at face value all attributions, assigned those documents to the period in which the Mishnah took shape, that is, the second century. Furthermore, in the theory that the laws of the Mishnah were generated by exegesis of Scripture—a theory advanced for the first time in the exegetical works of the Mishnah itself—it was commonly imagined that the so-called Tannaitic midrashim (that is, exegeses of Scripture attributed to Mishnah authorities called Tannas) go "way back." These propositions lose all credibility if we do not assume that everything attributed to an authority really was said by him, and if we recognize, as we must, that the Mishnah is quoted verbatim in these writings, and, more important, that the Mishnah forms the agenda for the authorship of these documents. While the generality of scholarship, represented for example by M. D. Heer's article, "Midrash," in *Encyclopaedia Judaica,* accepts the fact that the so-called Tannaitic midrashim are post-Mishnaic, however, we have no clear dates for the compilations of those books. The earliest point that seems probable is 300, the latest, sometime in relationship to the Yerushalmi (Talmud of the Land of Israel) in ca. 400–450. On that basis the statement here is made; but it is not so firm a basis as the others.

The fact that the changes exposed in the writings emerging at the end of the fourth century met head-on the Christian challenge is shown in a separate book of mine, *Judaism and Christianity in the Age of Constantine: Issues in the Initial Confrontation* (Chicago: University of Chicago Press, 1987). There I show that the doctrines of history, the Messiah, and the identification of Israel framed in significant fourth-century Church Fathers and in the writings of the sages of the same period form counterparts and opposites, each side addressing precisely the agenda framed by the other and confronting head-on the claim of the other. I compare the doctrine of history of Eusebius with that Genesis Rabbah; the doctrine of the Messiah of Chrysostom with that of the Talmud of the Land of Israel; and the doctrine of who is Israel of Aphrahat with that of Leviticus Rabbah and Genesis Rabbah. I further show that matters unaffected by the intellectual confrontation of Christian theologians and Judaic sages, exegesis of Scripture, on the one side, the canonization of holy writings, on the other, find the two parties totally out of relationship with one another: different people talking about different things to different people. So where the two sides talked about the same things, I maintain, it was because the politics of the time forced them to. That quite separate book contributes its evidence to the proposition presented for the first time here.

Judaism was born in the matrix of Christianity because the Judaism of the dual Torah, coming to its first systematic and complete statement in the pages of the Talmud of the Land of Israel, came forth as offspring of the Christianity of the fourth century. The system in its first distinctive formulation presented a point-by-point response to an unprecedented challenge of a very particular character. Sharing the Torah of Israel, therefore claiming the attention of Israel's sages, and with the political power to make that claim stick, Christianity spoke of the Messiah now King, of the cross now in the heavens, of the ineluctable meaning and message of the Old Testament, of Rome as God's instrument through the Christian emperors. And the Judaism of the dual Torah took full and ample note of the message, hence, Judaism in the matrix of Christianity. And it was a Judaism that enjoyed remarkable success in Christendom, answering the urgent question of Christianity with a response of, to Jews, self-evident and compelling power: God loves Israel, the Jewish people, and the Torah is the symbol of that love. What made all the difference in the hundred years prior to the closing of the Talmud of the Land of Israel in ca. 400 C.E., Genesis Rabbah and Leviticus Rabbah sometime thereafter, and Sifra and Sifre to Numbers and to Deuteronomy at an indeterminate point possibly between 300 and 400, therefore, was the political triumph marked by the passage of Christianity from persecuted to established religion, dated with the toleration of Christianity after 312 to the Code of Theodosius at the end of the century. At that time the points of challenge addressed to the Judaic sages of the Land of Israel by Christianity found a response. Christianity read the same Scriptures, and sages responded with a systematic exegesis of the passages of those Scriptures they deemed central. Christianity produced its encompassing symbol, and sages provided a counterpart for Judaism. Christianity raised the question of the Messiah and the meaning of history, and sages responded. Christianity now dominant in Rome changed the character of the empire, and sages replied with a theory of Rome as Esau, Ishmael, Edom: part of the family, but the wrong part.

Judaism without Christianity is represented by the Mishnah and its close associates, Abot and the Tosefta: stress on sanctification, a politics of accommodation. These two definitive traits of the Judaism of the dual Torah persisted unchanged, since the politics to which they responded—the circumstance of a defeated nation, living in its own land to be sure—had not changed. The other four traits we shall trace through the canonical writings all made their shift within the pages of the Talmud of the Land of Israel, and, I shall argue, the reason for the change derived from the remarkable political revolution of the fourth century. So to conclude: the Judaic system adumbrated by the Mishnah and its closest continuators, Abot and the Tosefta, formed *a Judaism without Christianity*. The Judaic system exposed by the Talmud of the Land of Israel and its closest friends, Genesis Rabbah and Leviticus Rabbah, constituted *a Judaism despite Christianity*. And that Judaism thrived in Christendom, sometimes under conditions of persecution, always under circumstances of subordination, and, because the fundamental political ecology remained constant, also in Islam. Only with the advent of a world in which the propositions of Christianity and Islam did not form self-evident truths did the Judaism of the dual Torah also lose that quality of self-evidence that had for fifteen hundred years made it normative Judaism for nearly all Jews everywhere. But the story of the Judaic systems formed in the encounter with an other-than-Christian or other-than-Islamic world I tell elsewhere.[2]

JACOB NEUSNER
Brown University

---

2. In *Death and Birth of Judaism* (New York: Basic Books, 1987), and, for the whole story, *Self-Fulfilling Prophecy: Exile and Return as the History of Judaism* (Boston: Beacon Press, 1987).

Acknowledgments

I enjoyed more than routine counsel and advice from Professor William Scott Green, University of Rochester, who saw in the essays I collect here that larger focus which, to begin with, I had missed. I perceived the whole as an exercise in constancy and change, missing what is in fact the point of the change: an exercise in the study of the ecology of a religion. I gladly express my indebtedness and thanks to Mr. Green for the hard and exceptionally perceptive work he put into this book.

I express my thanks also to the staff of Fortress Press for yet another encounter of a most gracious and professional character. Dr. Harold Rast, the director, and Dr. Davis Perkins, my editor for this project, maintained the remarkable standard of Fortress Press for collegiality joined to constructive criticism and expressed in a generous and affectionate spirit. I have been unusually fortunate in my experience with editors in various presses of an academic, religious, and trade character, and I can remember only the most cordial and gratifying experiences in publishing books for twenty-five years. Yet among them all Fortress under its present leadership truly distinguishes itself and I am thankful.

Introduction

The Ecology of Religion and the Case of Judaism

This is a book about the ecology of religion, meaning that it is about the interplay between a religious system and the world that gives it shape and meaning. This intends to exemplify in a very particular setting the larger problem of how to relate the content of a religion to its context, culture to conviction, and above all, social change (which is public and general) to symbol change (which is particular and distinctive to its setting). We deal in particular with the extraordinary shift in the symbolic structure of Judaism represented by writings brought to closure at the end of the fourth century and the beginning of the fifth in the Land of Israel. These writings show that the canon of a particular Judaic religious system (hence, a Judaism), the definition of the system's teleology, and the designation of the use and meaning of the system's encompassing symbol all changed. Why the change matters is simple. The Judaic canon, its teleology, and its symbolic structure in the period at hand reached a definition that all three would know up to the present day. If we define Judaism as the religion of the dual Torah, written and oral, aimed at the salvation brought by the coming of the Messiah in response to the sanctification of Israel, expressed by the encompassing and governing system of Torah—thus canon, teleology, and symbol—then we identify the fourth century as the point at which that Judaism emerged in the writings of the faith. The upshot is simple. While Christianity began in the matrix of Ju-

1

daism in the first century, Judaism reached its present definition in the matrix of Christianity in the fourth.

In this book I draw upon a metaphor from the natural sciences for the study of religion. Ecology is a branch of science concerned with the interrelationships of organisms and their environments. By "ecology of" is meant, the study of the interrelationship between a particular religious way of viewing the world and living life, and the historical, social, and especially political situation of the people who view the world and live life in accord with the teachings of their religion. The Jewish people form a very small group, spread over many countries. One fact of their natural environment is that they form a distinct group in diverse societies. A second is that they constitute solely a community of fate and, for many, of faith, in that they have few shared social or cultural traits. A third is that they do not form a single political entity. A fourth is that they look back upon a very long and in some ways exceptionally painful history. A worldview suited to the Jews' social ecology must make sense of their unimportance and explain their importance. It must explain the continuing life of the group and persuade people that their forming a distinct and distinctive community is important and worth perpetuating. The interplay between the political, social, and historical life of the Jews and their conceptions of themselves in this world and the next—that is, their worldview contained in their canon, their way of life, explained by the teleology of the system, and the symbolic structure that encompasses the two and stands for the whole all at once and all together—defines the focus for the inquiry into the ecology of the religion at hand. Thus we have the ecology of Judaism.

In point of fact the ecology of Judaism in its formative century finds definition in the ecology of Christianity in the century that marks the first in its history as the formative power in the history of the West: the fourth century. Judaism and Christianity interrelate intensely and continuously from the beginning to the present. As said at the outset, everyone knows that Christianity came into being within the matrix of Judaism. But it also is the fact that Judaism came into being within the matrix of Christianity. Christianity began its life on earth within Israel, the Jewish people, and for a long time remained a kind of Judaism. It never gave up the claim to carry forward the revelation to Israel by God at Sinai. Judaism would live out its history within two worlds: first the Christian and later the Muslim. But it was in the former, the Christian, that Judaism as it would emerge from late antiquity reached that definition that would prove characteristic from then to now. In the definition of each of its systemically definitive characteristics—canon, teleology, symbol—Judaism found its points of emphasis and stress in the ecology framed by Christianity at its moment of triumph.

In the fourth century the religious worlds of the West—the worlds of Judaism and Christianity—changed places. The one nurtured in active politics became apolitical, leaving the world of history. The other, born on the fringes of empire, took control of the government of the world. Judaism, prepared for one politics, now addressed a people without politics. Christianity, born among the weak and subjugated, turned out to rule the world. The ecology of each drastically shifted.

All Christianities—the set of related religious systems, worldviews, and ways of life addressed to a distinctive social group that took shape around the crucifixion and resurrection of Christ—took for granted a single fact. This world lay in the charge of others, not Christians. The Christian's duty in this life directed attention to the next. Imitating Christ for some required martyrdom, for others acts of exemplary kindness. For none could imagine what actually would take place: a Rome become Christian. The corresponding Judaisms shared the opposite premise. Israel constituted a this-worldly and political entity, whatever other ranges of existence beyond and within may have defined vistas for consideration. So Christianities and Judaisms concurred, each on its own side of the line of politics and government, history and power: the one made no provision for rule, the other took it for granted. In the fourth century the two sets of systems changed positions. For the West this change has made all the difference.

When under Constantine the religious systems of Christianity became licit, then favored, and finally dominant in the government of the Roman Empire, Christians confronted a world for which nothing had prepared them. But they did not choose to complain. For the political triumph of Christ, now ruler of the world in dimensions wholly unimagined, brought its own lessons. All of human history required fresh consideration, from the first Adam to the last. The writings of churches now asked to be sorted out so that the canon, Old and New, might correspond to the standing and clarity of the new Christian situation. So too one powerful symbol, the cross selected by Constantine for his army and by which he won, took a position of dominance and declared its distinctive message of a Christianity in charge of things. Symbol, canon, and systemic teleology responded to the unprecedented circumstance of Christ on the throne of the nations.

At the end of that century of surprises, in the year 429 the Jews of the Land of Israel for their part confronted a situation without precedent. That year marked the end of the patriarchal government that had ruled the Jews of the Land of Israel for the preceding three centuries. It was the end of their political entity, their instrument of self-administration and government in their own land. Tracing its roots back for centuries and claiming to originate in the family of David, the Jewish government (that of the patriarch), had succeeded the regime of the priests in the Temple and the kings, first allies, then agents of Rome on their throne. Israel's tradition of government of course went back to Sinai. No one had ever imagined that the Jews would define their lives other than together as a people, a political society, with collective authority and shared destiny and a public interest. The revelation of Sinai addressed a nation, the Torah gave laws to be kept and enforced, and Israel found definition in comparison to other nations. It would have rulers, subject to God's authority to be sure, and it would have a king now and a king-messiah at the end of time. So the fourth century brought a hitherto unimagined circumstance: an Israel lacking the authority to rule itself under its own government, even the ethnic and patriarchal one that had held things together on the other side of the end of long centuries of priestly rule in the Temple and royal rule in Jerusalem.

In effect the two systems had prepared for worlds that neither would inhabit: the one for the status of governed, not governor, the other for the opposite. Christianity in politics would define not the fringes but the very fabric of society and culture. Judaism out of politics altogether would find its power in the donated obedience of people in no way to be coerced except from within or from on high. Whatever "Christianity" and "Judaism" would choose as their definition beyond the time of turning, therefore, would constitute mediating systems that responded to a new world out of an inappropriate old. The Judaism that would take shape beyond the fourth century, beginning in writings generally thought to have come to closure at the end of that momentous age, would use writings produced in one religious ecological system to address a quite different one; so too would the Christianity that would rule, both in its Western and in its Eastern expressions.

This book takes up the description of how a particular religion took shape in response to an unprecedented challenge and so forms an exercise in the ecology of religion. At stake in this ecology of religion is the interpretation of how a religion emerges from one world to another and makes the painful passage from one age to another which enduring religions have to travel.

When we study religion we deal with what I believe to be the single most important force in the formation of the life of civilization. What we want to know about religion as exemplified by the ecology of Judaism, therefore, is how religion forms a force in society and politics. In asking about the political and social problem addressed by matters of belief—canon, teleology, symbol—we place religion at the center of the world of humanity in society. At stake in making the points at hand, therefore, is nothing less than the interpretation of the history of the West. This view of what we study when we study religion and this definition of what is at stake in religion contradict broadly held views. To illustrate why I claim to do something essentially different here, let me refer to those views of what matters in religion. Why does the ecology of religion refocus what we study when we study religion?

For the nearly four hundred years since the Lutheran Reformation and especially in the two hundred years since the Enlightenment, two powerful forces have worked to transform religion from the paramount force in public life such as I represent religion to be in this book—the formative force in culture and politics—into something else. Religion found itself turned into something private, beyond rational discourse, and therefore trivial and apolitical. Religion is a matter of belief and opinion—not knowledge. The secularists wished to force religion off the public stage, the theologians to keep it vivid in the heart of the individual. Together they worked to represent religion as private (Protestant) and trivial (secular), a matter of deep conscience

(Protestant) or personal caprice and beyond rational and critical inquiry (secular).

Though hardly a conspiracy, Protestant theology and militant secularism have formed a phalanx to drive religion off the stage of public cultural life and back into the corners of private life. Not a matter of public responsibility and shared discourse, religion for the secularist faded from consciousness. And the Protestants proved complicit. If, as Protestant theology in the Lutheran tradition maintained, true religion takes place in the heart, in the act of faith by which alone we are saved, then religion does not form a component of culture but a constituent of conscience. Religion found itself forced from the public stage because it was private, a matter of caprice, and in the end, trivial. God speaks, it turned out, in so many individual voices that we hear only a cacophony, not a social message at all. When people study religion today, they learn implicitly that it is self-evidently a matter of personal theological conviction.

But because of religion nations make war or peace. Because of religion people give their lives. Because of religion economic decisions favor one course of action and not some other. Politics, culture, social organization form a single cogent system in country after country because of religion. Wherever we turn, from Europe to the Middle East to India to the South Pacific to the outer reaches of the Soviet Empire itself, religion turns out to form the single force that defines reality for humankind. It is neither private nor trivial but public, political, and determinative. Most of the world is what it is today because of religion.

According to the opposite view, in religion there is something to be reported and recorded but not studied. The study of religion—within this theory—does not involve knowledge of the world or even of the self as representative of other selves, but only of the individual at the most unique and unrepresentative. If God speaks to me in particular then the message by definition is mine—not yours. Religion, the totality of these private messages (within the present theory), therefore does not make itself available for study and analysis, for communication in public discourse, and that too is by definition. So within this theological theory of the matter there is slight basis for academic study for there is nothing to know, only something to report for the appreciation and edification of others. "Thus saith the Lord"—to me in particular. The mighty accumulation of such messages may impress, but hardly informs in the way in which we receive and analyze information in the academy.

My premise in this book is the opposite: when we study the ecology of religion we study how humanity in society responded to challenge and change, mediated between the received tradition of politics and social life and the crisis of the age and circumstance. Religion is not trivial, not private, not individual, not a matter of the heart. Religion is public, political, social, economic. It is not possible to understand the world today without grasping the reality of religion as a powerful force in shaping politics and culture, economic action and social organization. That is a fact. No single object of study forms so public and social—indeed so measurable—a presence as religion.

In this book, therefore, I propose to treat religion in a way contrary to the prevailing attitude of mind which identifies religion with belief to the near-exclusion of behavior. The prevailing attitude of mind suggests that we ask not about society but self, not about culture and community but about conscience and character. So when people study religion they tend in the aggregate to speak of individuals and not groups: faith and its substance and, beyond faith, the things that faith represents: faith reified, hence, religion. As William Scott Green states:

> The basic attitude of mind characteristic of the study of religion holds that religion is certainly in your soul, likely in your heart, perhaps in your mind, but never in your body. That attitude encourages us to construe religion cerebrally and individually, to think in terms of beliefs and the believer, rather than in terms of behavior and community. The lens provided by this prejudice draws our attention to the intense and obsessive belief called "faith," so religion is understood as a state of mind, the object of intellectual or emotional commitment, the result of decisions to believe or to have faith. According to this model, people have religion but they do not do their religion. Thus we tend to devalue behavior and performance, to make it epiphenomenal, and of course to emphasize thinking and reflecting, the practice of theology, as a primary activity of religious people. . . . The famous slogan that "ritual recapitulates myth" follows this model by assigning priority to the story and to peoples' believing the story, and makes behavior simply an imitation, an aping, a mere acting out.[1]

1. Personal letter, January 17, 1985.

What is at stake here is the definition of religion or rather what matters in religion, emerging from Protestant theology and Protestant religious experience. For when we lay heavy emphasis on faith to the exclusion of works, on the individual rather than on society, conscience instead of culture, we simply adopt as normative for academic scholarship convictions critical to the Protestant Reformation. Judaism and the historical, classical forms of Christianity, Roman Catholic and Orthodox, place emphasis at least equally on religion as a matter of works and not faith alone, behavior and community as well as belief and conscience. Religion is something that people do, and they do it together. Religion is not something people merely have as individuals. Since the entire civilization of the West from the fourth century carried forward the convictions of Christianity, not about the individual alone but about politics and culture, we may hardly find surprising the Roman Catholic conviction that religion flourishes not only in heart and mind but in eternal social forms: the Church in former times and the state as well. But for the social and cultural dimensions of religion the present academic sciences of religion find little space. Green sheds further light on the matter:

> The Protestant prejudice encourages us not to listen to what people actually say and not to watch what they actually do, but to suppose that these tractables are mere reflections of some underlying belief that is the ultimate grounding of the religious life. We need to reshape our collective curiosity and transcend the boundaries of this intellectual prejudice to acquire a fuller picture of the richness of religions as they are lived, acted, and performed—that is, to understand religions as we find them.[2]

As Green says, our intense interest in religion as faith instead of religion as social fact and cultural determinant derives from our origins in Protestant theology as that theology took shape at a particular moment in the history of American Protestant thought on the one side, and American culture on the other.

If we concur that we cannot understand the record of humanity without paying close attention to religion, then we should want to know about religion with precision and specificity. Our principal concern should not be whether religions are "right" or "wrong," but with

2. Personal letter, January 17, 1985.

what religion is, how it works, what difference it makes in politics and social life, economic action and cultural expression. When we study religion we nevertheless also want to know about its intellectual aspect, and that is a critical focus of this book. But the teachings of religion come to us in books, not in the personal feelings or opinions of this believer or that one, and the canon presents the faith, not the heart of the individual believer (except, to be sure, after the fact). When theologians treat religion as personal they do no less to trivialize religion than when secularists treat it as private. Religion as arbiter of culture and source of the values of politics and economy alike defines the public life of humanity. As such it is subject to description, reasoned analysis, and rigorous interpretation.

It is with these methodological presuppositions in mind that we examine Judaism at a moment of radical change, a moment of change more compelling than the destruction of the Temple. The Christianization of the Roman Empire presented Jews with a challenge more severe than the destruction of the Temple. The reason? Christianity claimed to be Judaism, Christians to be Israel. More subtle and more insidious, the challenge of Christianity addressed not the frontiers of the people from without but the soul and heart of the people from within. The shift in the condition of Israel marked by Christ's rise to political power and the Torah's loss of a place in political institutions has defined the context of Judaism from then to nearly the present day. And it must be said that the response of the day—represented by the Judaism defined in the documents of the late fourth and fifth centuries—proved remarkably successful. Judaism did endure. So in the shifts in the symbolic system represented by the redefinitions of canon, teleology, and encompassing symbol, the Judaism that emerged from the fourth century, principally in the pages of the Talmud of the Land of Israel, and two hundred years later reached fruition in the Talmud of Babylonia, enjoyed stunning success. We want to know whether and how the Judaism for which we have data changed in the context of the creation of the Christian culture. We shall find out that Judaism did change and that Christianity made a considerable difference in the change.

Judaism as we know it, that type of Judaism built upon the doctrine of the dual Torah, oral and written, revealed to Moses by God at

Sinai, took shape between the first and the seventh centuries. During that long period of time—a longer span than the one separating us from Columbus—the great structure rose in stages. In this book we consider three important changes in the formative history of Judaism as well as two significant aspects of constancy in that same historical period. Specifically, we consider change in the mode of preserving scriptural interpretation, in the mode of symbolizing the faith and system as a whole, and in the mode of framing and symbolizing the system's teleology. We contrast these critical changes in the system with two quite different matters in which we discover no change at all. The matter of what remains constant proves more complicated. Some classifications produce no marks of change because in the system at hand they bore no weight or meaning. Others yield quite uniform treatment, beginning to end, because the system had no fresh message to deliver. But most interestingly, there are central doctrines of Judaism that reveal no mark of change because the social foundations of the system, on the basis of which we should anticipate change to be generated, remained stable.

Once we take account of important points of constancy as well as significant aspects of change, we ask the central question of this book. It is in two parts. First, why do some things remain the same while others do not? Second, can we identify a point at which symbol changes of various kinds converge? A theory in response to the first of the two questions lays the foundations for a theory in reply to the second.

In chapter 2 I argue, on the basis of the persistence of the Priestly mode of viewing the world, that a continuing and deeply rooted social problem will lead to the persistence among diverse groups of a single structure of culture and faith. Asking what draws together the framers of the Priestly Code and its larger worldview as well as the founders of the Essene and Pharisaic movements of a much later period, I respond with the thesis that symbol change corresponds to social change, and that the stability of symbols bespeaks the persistence of a chronic social condition. In Part 3 I ask at what point we discern the changes that mark the movement from what I call the Mishnaic form of Judaism to the Talmudic Judaism that emerges as dominant at the end of the formation of Judaism. In looking at the shifts traced in chapters 6, 7, and 8, time and again a convergence of lines of change at a single moment is found, in one document. It is in the fourth century in the Talmud of the Land of Israel which reached closure, scholars generally concur, at about 400 C.E. What then characterized the fourth century? For the Land of Israel where the Talmud took shape it was, of course, the triumph of Christianity, first with Constantine's conversion and recognition as licit the long-persecuted church, then with his heirs' establishment of Christianity as most favored, and finally, as the official faith of the Roman Empire. When I reexamine each of the foci of change—hermeneutical, symbolic, and teleological—I discover a single interesting convergence: each doctrine in Judaism responds to a point of contention with Christianity.

On that basis the hypothesis is offered that the fourth century in point of fact marks the birth of Judaism, or as we should state matters, the fourth century is the first century of Judaism as we know it. It is everywhere understood that the fourth century also marks the first century of Christianity as the West would know it. Thus the first century for the Judaic and Christian West therefore was the fourth century. The social and political change to account for the enormous shifts in the history of the symbolic structure and system of Judaism in its canonical literature therefore occurred in the fourth century. When Rome became Christian, Judaism as it would flourish in Western civilization reached that familiar form and definition which we know today. Judaism was born in the matrix of Christianity triumphant or, to use theological language of a sort, Christ enthroned dictated not only the dominant faith but also the successful one (successful for reasons I suggest at the very end).

In this book I review and draw together the results of several prior studies, none of which contains the main ideas of the present work, but all of which contribute their fair share. Chapter 1 rests upon *Judaism: The Evidence of the Mishnah* (Chicago: University of Chicago Press, 1981). Chapters 6, 7, and 8 draw their main points from my *Foundations of Judaism: Method, Teleology, Symbol* series (Philadelphia: Fortress Press) which consists of three volumes, *Midrash in*

Context (1983), *Messiah in Context* (1984), and *Torah* (1985). Chapter 4 depends upon *Vanquished Nation, Broken Spirit: The Virtues of the Heart in Formative Judaism* (Cambridge: Cambridge University Press, forthcoming). I have put everything together in a new way to produce the thesis of this book.

PART ONE

SYMBOL CHANGE
AND
SOCIAL CHANGE

1

The Fourth Century as the True First Century in the History of the Judaic and Christian West

In hermeneutics, symbolic structure, and teleology, the changes characteristic of the fourth- and early fifth-century components of the canon of Judaism contrast strikingly with the stability in the doctrine of emotions and the symbolization of the outsider, characteristic of that same canon. A theory that explains why the one changed must account also for the constancy of the other.

In my view of the reason that some things underwent radical revision while others did not derives from the particular character of change fundamental in the politics and social life of the Land of Israel as of the rest of the Roman East marked by the fourth century. When Rome became Christian, the condition of Israel changed in some ways but not in others. What remained the same? The politics and social context of a defeated nation. What changed? The circumstance and context of the religious system of Judaism. The situation of *Israel* did not change. The setting of *Judaism* did. How so? Israelites in the Land of Israel persisted as a subject-people. But Judaism now confronted a world in which its principal components—hermeneutic, teleology, symbol—confronted an effective challenge in the corresponding components of the now-triumphant faith in Christ.

Specifically, the Hebrew Scriptures, the written Torah, now demanded a reading as the Old Testament predicting the New. Why? Because history now proved that Scripture's prophetic promises of a king-messiah had pointed toward Jesus, now Christ enthroned. Concomitantly the teleology of the Israelite system of old, focused as it was on the coming of the Messiah, now found confirmation and realization in the rule of Jesus—again, Christ enthroned. And the symbol of the whole—hermeneutics, teleology alike—rose in heaven's heights: the cross that had triumphed at the Milvian Bridge. No wonder that the three critical components of the Mishnaic system of Judaism now came under sharp revision. The written Torah found completion in the oral one. So Judaism's extra-scriptural traditions found legitimacy. The system as a whole pointed toward an eschatological teleology to be realized in the coming of the Mishnah when Israel's condition itself warranted. The symbol of the Torah expanded to encompass the teleology and hermeneutic at hand. Salvation comes from the Torah, not the cross. So point by point the principles of Judaism manifest in the fresh reading of the Talmud of the Land of Israel, which reached closure at the end of the fourth century, responded point by point to the particular challenge of the principal event of that century.

So the fourth century marked the first century of Judaism as it would flourish in the West. It further indicated the first century of Christianity as Christianity enthroned would define and govern the civilization of the West. This thesis demands exposition and demonstration and I here offer it in a preliminary way. My intent is to account for the points of change and stability revealed in the canonical history of ideas we now survey. Christianity accounts for change in Judaism. Social and political stability explain the constancy of those symbols or modes of symbolic behavior that do not change in Israel.

Let us review briefly what mattered to Israel in the Land of Israel in the history of the fourth century, beginning with Constantine's conversion and ending with the ultimate dissolution of the institutions and social foundations of paganism.

Since the fundamental shifts in the symbolic system appear at one point, namely, in the movement from the Mishnah and its nearby exegetical and apologetic literature to the Talmuds (and in particular to the Yerushalmi), we turn our gaze to the fourth century. We ask for details of what happened to redefine Israel's social and political circumstances so radically. Obviously the answer for the Land of Israel was the same in the fourth century as it was in the second. The change that marked the advent of the Mishnah, a revolution in its age, was the same as the one that had accompanied the appearance of the Yerushalmi (viewed as a process that lasted approximately a century). It was a considerable political turning.

In both the second and the fourth centuries the matter reached full symbolic realization in the name by which the Land of Israel would be known. In the second century the Land of Israel became "Palestine." Israel was defeated, so Rome renamed the Land. In the fourth century the Land of Israel became, for Christian Rome that ruled, "the Holy Land." Israel was now vanquished in heaven as much as on earth, so triumphant Christianity would now rename the Land. But for Israel the Land of Israel would always be what it was from the beginning, and what it is once more in our day, namely, the Land of Israel, now the State if not the condition of Israel.

For nearly everyone in the Roman world the most important events of the fourth and fifth centuries (the period in which the Talmud of the Land of Israel and collections of exegeses such as Leviticus Rabbah were coming into being) were first, the legalization of Christianity followed very rapidly second, by the adoption of Christianity as the state's most favored religion and third, by the delegitimization of paganism and the systematic degradation of Judaism. The astonishing advent of legitimacy and even power provoked Christian intellectuals to rewrite Christian and world history and work out theology as a reflection on this new polity and its meaning in the unfolding of human history. A new commonwealth was coming into being, taking over the old and reshaping it for the new age. In 312 Constantine achieved power in the West. In 323 he took the government of the entire Roman Empire into his own hands. He promulgated the edict of Milan in 313, whereby Christianity attained the status of toleration. Christians and all others were given "the free power to follow the religion of their choice." In the next decade Christianity became the most favored religion. Converts from Judaism were protected and could not be punished by Jews. Christians were freed of the obligation to perform pagan sacrifices. Priests were exempted from certain taxes. Sunday became an obligatory day of rest. Celibacy was permitted. From 324 onward Constantine ceased to maintain a formal impartiality, now intervening in the affairs of the Church, settling quarrels among believers, and

calling the Church Council at Nicaea (325) to settle issues of the faith.
He was baptized on the eve of his death in 337. Over the next century
the pagan cults were destroyed, their priests deprived of support, their
intellectuals bereft of standing.

So far as the Jews of the Land of Israel were concerned, not much
changed at the Milvian Bridge in 312 when Constantine conquered
in the sign of Christ. The sages' writings nowhere refer explicitly to
that event. They scarcely gave testimony to its consequences for the
Jews and continued to harp upon prohibited relationships with "pagans" in general, as though nothing had changed from the third century to the fourth and fifth. Legal changes affecting the Jews under
Constantine's rule indeed were not substantial. Jews could not pros-
elytize; they could not circumcise slaves when they bought them; Jews
could not punish other Jews who became Christians. Jews, finally,
were required to serve on municipal councils wherever they lived, an
onerous task involving responsibility for collecting taxes. But those
who served synagogues, patriarchs, and priests were still exempted
from civil and personal obligations. In the reign of Constantius III
(337–361) further laws aimed at separating Jews from Christians were
enacted in 339 in the Canons of Elvira. These forbade intermarriage
between Jews and Christians, further protected converts, and forbade
Jews to hold slaves of Christian or other gentile origin.

The reversion to paganism on the part of Emperor Julian, ca. 360,
involved a measure of favor to Jews and Judaism. To embarrass Christianity he permitted the rebuilding of the Temple at Jerusalem, but he
died before much progress could be made. In the aftermath of the
fiasco of Julian's reversion to paganism, the Christians returning to
power determined to make certain such a calamity would never recur.
Accordingly, over the next century they undertook a sustained attack
on institutions and personnel of paganism in all its expressions. The
long-term and systematic effort in time overspread Judaism as well.
From the accession of Theodosius II in 383 to the death of his son
Arcadius in 408, Judaism came under attack. In the earlier part of the
fifth century, Jews' rights and the standing of their corporate communities were substantially affected. The patriarchate of the Jews of
the Land of Israel, the ethnarch and his administration, was abolished.
So from the turn of the fifth century, the government policy was meant

to isolate Jews, lower their status, and suppress their agencies of self-rule.

Laws against intermarriage posed no problem to the Jews. The ones limiting proselytism and those protecting converts from Judaism did not affect many people. But the edicts that reduced Jews to second-class citizenship did matter. They were not to hold public office but still had to sit on city councils responsible for the payment of taxes. Later they were removed from the councils though still obligated, of course, for taxes. Between 404 and 438 Jews were forbidden to hold office in the civil service, represent cities, and serve in the army or at the bar, and they ultimately were evicted from every public office. The period from Julian's fall onward, moreover, presented Israel with problems of a profoundly religious character.

There were five events of fundamental importance for the history of Judaism in the fourth and fifth centuries. All of them except for the last were well known in their day. These were as follows: (1) the conversion of Constantine; (2) the fiasco of Julian's plan to rebuild the Temple of Jerusalem; (3) the depaganization of the Roman Empire, a program of attacks on pagan temples and, along the way, synagogues; (4) the Christianization of the majority of the population of Palestine; and (5) the creation of the Talmud of the Land of Israel and of compositions of scriptural exegeses. The Talmud and the exegetical compilations came into being in an age of crisis, high hope, and then disaster. Vast numbers of Jews now found chimerical the messianic expectation, as they had framed it around Julian's plan to rebuild the Temple. A time of boundless expectations was followed by one of bottomless despair.

Let us briefly review the four events that framed the setting for the fifth, starting with Constantine's conversion. The first point is that we do not know how Jews responded to Constantine's establishment of Christianity as the most favored religion. But in the Land of Israel itself his works were well known, since he and his mother purchased many sites believed connected with Israel's sacred history and built churches and shrines at them. They rewrote the map of the Land of Israel. Every time they handled a coin, moreover, Jews had to recognize that something of fundamental importance had shifted, for the old pagan images were blotted out as Christian symbols took their place.

A move of the empire from reverence for Zeus to adoration of
Mithra meant nothing to the Jew; paganism was what it was, lacking
all differentiation in the Jewish eye. Christianity was different. Why?
Because it was like Judaism. Christians read the Torah and claimed
to declare its meaning. Accordingly, the trend of the sages' speculation
cannot have avoided the issue of the place within the Torah's messianic
pattern of the remarkable turn in world history represented by the
triumph of Christianity. Since Christians vociferously celebrated their
faith in Christ's messiahship and at the moment Jews were hardly
prepared to concur, it surely falls within known patterns for us to
suppose that Constantine's conversion would have been identified with
some dark moment to prefigure the dawning of the messianic age.

Second, if people were then looking for a brief dawn, Emperor Julian's plan to rebuild the ruined Temple in Jerusalem must have dazzled
their eyes. For while Constantine surely raised the messianic question,
for a brief hour Emperor Julian appeared decisively to answer it. In
361 the now-pagan Julian gave permission to rebuild the Temple.
Work briefly got under way, but stopped because of an earthquake.
The intention of Julian's plan was quite explicit. Julian meant to falsify
the prophecy of Jesus that "not one stone of the temple would be left
upon another." We may take for granted that since Christ's prophecy
had not been proven false, many surely concluded that it indeed had
now been shown true. We do not know that Jews in numbers then
drew the conclusion that, after all, Jesus really was the Christ. Many
Christians said so. But in the next half-century Palestine gained a
Christian majority. Christians were not slow to claim their faith had
been proved right. We need not speculate on the depth of disappoint-
ment felt by those Jews who had hoped that the project would come
to fruition and herald the Messiah they awaited instead of the Christian one.

Third, the last pagan emperor's threat to Christianity made urgent
the delegitimization of paganism. In the formation of a new and ag-
gressive policy toward outsiders Judaism, too, was caught in the net.
To be sure, Jews were to be protected but degraded. The sword un-
sheathed against the pagan cult-places was sharp but untutored. It was
not capable of discriminating among non-Christian centers of divine
service. Nor could those who wielded it, zealots of the faith in church

and street, have been expected to do so. The non-Christian Roman government protected synagogues and punished those who damaged them. Its policy was to extirpate paganism but protect a degraded Judaism. But the faithful of the church had their own ideas. Their assault against pagan temples spilled over into an ongoing program of attacking synagogue property.

That long-established Roman tradition of toleration of Judaism and of Jews, extending back to the time of Julius Caesar and applying both in law and in custom, now drew to a close. A new fact, at this time lacking all basis in custom and in the policy of state and church alike, faced Jews: physical insecurity in their own villages and towns. Jews' synagogues and homes housed the same thing that was to be eradicated: Judaism. A mark of exceptional piety came to consist in violence against Jews' holy places, their property and persons. Coming in the aftermath of the triumph of Christianity on the one side, and the decisive repudiation of the Jews' hope for the rebuilding of the Temple on the other, was the hitherto-unimagined war against the Jews. In the last third of the fourth century and the beginning of the fifth this war raised once again those questions about the meaning of the history that Constantine at the beginning of the age at hand had forced upon Israel's consciousness.

Fourth, at this time there seems to have been a sharp rise in the numbers of Christians in the Holy Land. Christian refugees from the West accounted for part of the growth. But there are stories about how Jews converted as well. The number of Christian towns and villages dramatically increased. If Jews did convert in sizeable numbers, then we should have to point to the events of the preceding decades as ample validation in their eyes for the Christian interpretation of history. Jews had waited nearly three hundred years from the destruction of the Temple in 70 for the promise of Julian. Instead of being falsified, however, Jesus' prophecy had been validated. No stone had been left on stone in the Temple, not after 70, not after 361, just as Jesus had said. Instead of a rebuilt temple the Jews looked out on a world in which now even their synagogues came under threat and, along with them, their own homes and persons. What could be more ample proof of the truth of the Christians' claim than the worldly triumph of their Church? Resisted for so long, that claim called into question (as in the time of Bar Kokba) whether it was worth waiting any longer for a Messiah who did not come when he was most needed. With followers proclaiming the Messiah who *had* come now possessing the world, the question could hardly be avoided.

Now that we understand the context, we appreciate the issues at hand. What happened was a world-historical change, one that could not be absorbed into Israel's available system of theories on the outsiders in general and the meaning of the history of the great empires in particular. The Christian empire was fundamentally different from its predecessor in two ways. First, it shared with Israel reverence for exactly the same Holy Scriptures on which Jewry based its existence. So it was no longer an entirely alien empire that ruled over the horizon. It was now a monotheist, formerly persecuted, biblical empire and not very different from Israel in its basic convictions about important matters of time and eternity. Second, the established policies of more than a half a millennium, from the time of the Maccabees' alliance with Rome to the start of the fourth century, now gave way. Tolerance of Judaism and an accommodation with the Jews in their Land—disrupted only by the Jews' own violation of the terms of the agreement in 70 and 132—now no longer obtained.

Jews surely had to wonder whether history was headed in the right direction and whether indeed the Christians, emerging from within Israel itself, may not initially have been right. The Empire now was Christian and Israel's most recent bout with messianic fever had proved disastrous. Julian's Temple had not been built. If, as was surely the case, some Jews thought that the building of that Temple would mean the Messiah was near at hand—or in fact had come—then the failure to build the Temple meant the Messiah was not near or never would come in the way Jews expected. The requirement to construct an apologetics therefore emerged from the condition of Israel, whether or not Christian polemicists had a hearing among Jews.

If we inquire into what the sages did at that time the answer is clear. They composed the Talmud of the Land of Israel as we know it. They collected exegeses of Scripture and made them into systematic and sustained accounts of the meaning of the Pentateuch (assuming dates in these centuries, late third through early fifth, for Sifra, the two Sifres, Genesis Rabbah and Leviticus Rabbah).

When we recall what Christians had to say to Israel, we may find entirely reasonable the view that compiling scriptural exegeses constituted part of a Jewish apologetic response. For one Christian message had been that Israel "after the flesh" had distorted and continually misunderstood the meaning of what had been its own Scripture. Failing to read the Old Testament in the light of the New, the prophetic promises in the perspective of Christ's fulfillment of those promises, Israel "after the flesh" had lost access to God's revelation to Moses at Sinai. It is easy to imagine that a suitably powerful yet appropriately proud response would have two qualities. First, it would supply a complete account of what Scripture had meant and always must mean as Israel read it. Second, it would do so in such a way as not to dignify the position of the other side with the grace of an explicit reply at all.

The compilations of exegeses and the Yerushalmi accomplished at this time assuredly take up the challenge of restating the meaning of the Torah revealed by God to Moses at Mount Sinai. This the sages did in a systematic and thorough way. At the same time, if the charges of the other side precipitated the work of compilation and composition, the consequent collections in no way suggest that this is the case. The issues of the documents are always made to emerge from the inner life not even of Israel in general but of the sages' estate in particular. Scripture was thoroughly "rabbinized," as earlier it had been Christianized. None of this suggests the other side had won a response for itself. Only the net effect of these compilations—a complete picture of the whole, as Israel must perceive the whole of revelation—suggests the extraordinary utility of these apologetics.

It follows that the changes at the surface—in articulated doctrines of teleology, hermeneutics, and symbolism—responded to changes in the political condition of Israel as well as in the religious foundations of the politics of the day. Paganism had presented a different and simpler problem to the sages. Christianity's explicit claims, validated in world-shaking events of the age, demanded a reply. The sages of the Talmud of the Land of Israel provided it. So it is at those very specific points at which the Christian challenge met old Israel's worldview head-on that the sages' doctrines change from what they had been. What did Israel have to counterpoise to the cross? The Torah in the doctrine, first, of the status as oral and memorized revelation of the Mishnah, and, by implication, of other rabbinical writings. The Torah, moreover, in the encompassing symbol of Israel's salvation. The Torah, finally, in the person of the Messiah who, of course, would be a rabbi. The Torah in all three modes confronted the cross with its doctrine of the triumphant Christ, Messiah and king, ruler now of heaven and earth.

So what changed? Those components of the sages' worldview that now stood in direct confrontation with counterparts on the Christian side. What remained the same? Doctrines governing fundamental categories of Israel's social life to which the triumph of Christianity made no material difference.

And with what outcome? A stunning success for that society for which the sages and, in the sages' view, God cared so deeply: eternal Israel after the flesh. For Israel did endure in the Christian West, enjoying the secure conviction of constituting that Israel after the flesh to which the Torah continued to speak. How do we know the sages' Judaism won? Because when in turn Islam gained its victory, Christianity throughout the Middle East and North Africa gave way. But the sages' Judaism in those same vast territories retained the loyalty and conviction of the people of the Torah. The cross would rule only where the crescent and its sword did not. But the Torah of Sinai everywhere and always sanctified Israel in time and promised secure salvation for eternity. So Israel believed and so does Israel believe today.

An iron consensus has it that Christianity made no difference to Judaism, which went its own way scarcely deigning to recognize the new religion. That consensus is probably right for the first century. But it is profoundly wrong for the fourth. When in the aftermath of the Temple destruction in 70, the sages worked out a Judaism without a Temple and a cult; they produced the Mishnah, a system of sanctification focused on the holiness of the priesthood, the cultic festivals, the Temple and its sacrifices, as well as on the rules for protecting that holiness from levitical uncleanness (four of the six divisions of the Mishnah on a single theme). In the aftermath of the conversion of the Roman Empire to Christianity and the triumph of Christianity in the generation beyond Julian "the apostate," the sages worked out in the pages of the Talmud of the Land of Israel and in the exegetical compilations of the age a Judaism intersecting with the Mishnah's but essentially asymmetrical with it. They produced a system for salvation focused on the power of the sanctification of the holy people.

Before concentrating on the fourth century, let us stand back and examine the Judaism without a Temple that emerged in a world in which there was no Christianity. This Judaism did not find it necessary to advance a doctrine of the authority of Scripture. Furthermore, the systematic exegetical effort at linking the principal document, the Mishnah, to Scripture is interesting for what it took as its principal focus. The system of the Mishnah—a Judaism for a world in which Christianity played no considerable role—took slight interest in the Messiah and presented a teleology lacking all eschatological, therefore messianic, focus. It laid no considerable stress on the symbol of the Torah, though of course the Torah as a scroll, as a matter of status, and as revelation of God's will at Sinai, enjoyed prominence. This Judaism produced a document, the Mishnah, so independent of Scripture that when the authors wished to say what Scripture said, they chose to do so in their own words and in their own way. Whatever their intent it clearly did not encompass explaining to a competing Israel, heirs of the same Scriptures of Sinai, just what authority validated the document and how the document related to Scripture. So when we listen to the silences of the Mishnah as much as to its points of stress, we hear a single message. It is a message of a Judaism that answered a single encompassing question: what, in the aftermath of the destruction of the holy place and holy cult, remained of the sanctity of the holy caste, the priesthood, the holy land, and above all the holy people and its holy way of life. The answer: sanctity persists indelibly in Israel, the people, in its way of life, in its land, in its priesthood, in its food, in its mode of sustaining life, in its manner of procreating and so sustaining the nation. But that answer subsequently found itself absorbed within a successor-system with its own points of stress and emphasis. So we now turn to the Judaism that took shape beyond 70 but before Constantine's rise to power in 312 (though I regard the year 362, when Julian's Christian heir mounted the throne and established the primacy of Christianity in the West, as more decisive). So first we ask where Christianity made no difference, and then we shall consider when Christianity made all the difference in the world.

PART TWO

WHERE CHRISTIANITY
MADE
NO DIFFERENCE

2

Change Without Christianity: The Enduring Structure from the Priestly Code to the Mishnah

To describe the perennial system of sanctification we begin with the Mishnah as it emerged at the end of the second century C.E. If we describe the document in terms of the three principal groups whose topical programs dominate, we sort out tractates which present cogent treatments of a given subject of special interest to priests, scribes, and householders. Priests took a special interest in the conduct of the Temple cult in Jerusalem and in the disposition of the rations in food provided for the support of the priesthood. Scribes treated with unusual care rules governing the proper preparation and use of documents, for example, writs of divorce, contracts governing property-rights in marriage, and the like. Householders, heads of family-farm establishments, followed with concern rules governing real estate, the conduct of the farm in general, disposition of crops, the religious requirements governing the farming unit (and other households) on special occasions, and the like. Table 1 shows the tractates that cover the distinct topical program of each of these groups: the one a caste, the second a profession, the third an economic-social class.

The point of this taxonomy is easy to explain. We are able to distinguish among the tractates of the Mishnah and to point to the categorical traits of each one. While an argument may be made for including a given tractate in more than a single category, nonetheless the basic picture is orderly. We confront definitive topics emerging

29

TABLE 1

Tractates of Principal Concern to Priests: Temple and Cult	Tractates of Principal Concern to Scribes: Courts and Documents	Tractates of Principal Concern to Householders: Home and Farm
Demai	Ketubot	Peah
Terumot	Nedarim	Kilayim
Maaserot	Nazir	Orla
Maaser Sheni	Sotah	Shabbat
Hallah	Gittin	Erubin
Bikkurim	Qiddushin	Besah
Pesahim	Baba Qamma	Moed Qatan
Sheqalim	Baba Mesia	Kelim
Yoma	Baba Batra	Toharot
Sukkah	Sanhedrin	Niddah
Rosh Hashshanah	Makkot	Uqsin
Taanit	Shebuot	Berakhot
Megillah	Horayot	Abodah Zarah
Hagigah		
Yebamot		
Zebahim		
Menahot		
Hullin		
Bekorot		
Arakin		
Temurah		
Keritot		
Meilah		
Tamid		
Middot		
Qinnim		
Oholot		
Negaim		
Parah		
Miqvaot		
Makhshirin		
Zabim		
Tebul Yom		
Yadayim		

from programs of quite separate groups, responsive to topics of special interest to one group and not some other. Obviously every topic is important to all groups; that generality hardly requires specification. But for the person who wanted to know in particular the rules governing farming, in Peah, Kilayim, and Orlah he will have found those rules of greater practical import than the ones (which also affected him and which he also will have kept) on how to prepare a marriage contract, a writ of divorce, or a will, or on how to conduct a trial and to adjudicate among conflicting claims and confused transactions. The scribe may also have been a householder, just as the householder also was subject to the laws of distinctive concern to the scribe. But tractates formed around questions pressing for the one can have been secondary for the other group. That the same things are to be said of the priests, who may also have been scribes but who most certainly also were householders, is self-evident.

The priestly interest in the Mishnah's completed corpus finds definition not only topically but also in a mode of literary composition. A singular rhetorical style characterizes narratives of events in the priestly calendar and cult. Certain passages in the Mishnah expressive of priestly topics diverge from the standard formal and analytical style otherwise dominant in the Mishnah. These passages have one thing in common: to describe cultic procedures they resort to narrative style, telling what someone does or did, with a minimum of interruption for the familiar exercises of analytic problem-solving. There is no effort to phrase all laws on the conduct of the cult in the form of a narrative. But discussions of precisely what is done in a particular rite, for example, one of sacrifice or of any Temple liturgy, take the form of a tale. While we have ample discussion on the costs of the various pilgrim offerings, the whole discussion is in analytical discourse (*m. Hag.* 1:1ff.). The actual killing and disposition of the animals—what the priest and sacrificer really do—are not dealt with. That is why at that point we do *not* find the mode of discourse shifting into tale-telling. By contrast, when the Mishnah wishes to tell us about *how* a Passover offering is killed, or how the high priest carries out the laborious liturgy of the Day of Atonement, the document's framers resort solely to the narrative mode.

A catalogue of those passages in the Mishnah that shift from analysis and problem-solving to narrative story-telling follows. First come the stories of the conduct of the cult, that is, the daily whole offering and how it is prepared, as well as on special occasions. The narrative of how the daily whole offering is prepared and dealt with in tractate Tamid covers the ground of tractates Zebahim and Menahot and explains why in those tractates we do not have a counterpart for the meat and meal offerings, to tractate Menahot's attractive story of how the priests deal with the show bread from week to week. The collection and expenditure of the *sheqel*, a poll tax in support of the public offerings of the Temple and of the upkeep of the building and its personnel, are worked out through an extended narrative (*m. Sheq.* 3:1–4:9). The administrators of the Temple are named and the procedures are related, all in the storytelling style (*m. Sheq.* 5:1–7:8).

The conduct of the Temple rites involving the high priest on the Day of Atonement is presented wholly in narrative style (*m. Yoma* 1:1–7:5). This narrative clearly depends upon the tale of Leviticus 16 for order and meaning. Now all is told in present-tense language and descriptive tale-telling style. The rite of the *lulab* on the Temple mount when the first day of the Festival (Tabernacles) coincided with the Sabbath is spelled out in narrative style (*m. Suk.* 4:4). The same applies for the rite of the willow branch at the altar (*m. Suk.* 4:5–7), the water libation, and the playing of the flute and the celebration of the drawing of water for the water libation (*m. Suk.* 5:1–5). All of these are described rather than analyzed and the description takes the style of telling a story of how things were done.

The law of slaughtering and roasting the Passover offering is worked out in narrative form (*m. Pes.* 5:5–10). A narrative relates how the first sheaf of wheat is cut for the *omer* offering (*m. Men.* 10:2–5). The way in which the priests take the bread offering in and out of the sanctum is told as a story (*m. Men.* 11:7), as stated above. Bikkurim spells out the bringing of first fruits to the Temple priest. It includes a narrative account of how this is done (*m. Bik.* 2:2–6, 7–9). The conduct of burning the red cow is presented through a sustained narrative. Then, the story told, the same matter is reviewed through the analysis of cases which exemplify principles and their legal expression (*m. Par.* 3:1–1; 4:1–4). The prayers for rain and the liturgy of the community for a fast day are set forth in essentially narrative style, describing how things are done with very little analysis and much emphasis upon tale-telling (*m. Ta.* 1:1–7, 2:1–5). The involvement of the priestly watch for a given week is specified and narrated.

The second part of this brief catalogue takes up tales of priestly conduct of special rites; not public and sacrificial liturgies, but those required for individual cases and necessitating participation of priests with or without an actual blood rite. The purification rite of one afflicted with *sara^cat* (Leviticus 13—14) is recorded as a narrative (*m. Neg.* 14:1–3, 8–10). The Temple rite of administering the bitter water to a woman accused of adultery is presented as a story (*m. Sot.* 1:4; 2:1–3, 3:1–2, 4).

In both topical program and (to a lesser extent) rhetorical plan, therefore, components of the Mishnah as a whole—a majority of tractates for one thing—carry forward the plan and program of the Priestly Code of Scripture—that is, Leviticus chapters 1 through 15—as well as other pentateuchal sources deriving from Priestly authorship. The fact hardly presents a surprise when we turn back to the origins of the Mishnaic system as a whole. These we may trace back to the period—perhaps a century—before the destruction of the Second Temple in 70 c.e. At that point only portions of what we know as the final statement of the Mishnah had achieved expression in such a way as to enter the process of tradition that culminated in the complete system. These earliest components of the Mishnaic system occur in particular in the Mishnah's Division on Purity laws, one of the six which would constitute the Mishnah in its final form. Constituents of some of the other divisions also go back to this inaugural period in the make-up of the whole.

Let us now review the relevant results of this history of the formation of the laws of the Mishnah and then proceed to explain continuity in the topical program linking the founders of the Mishnah in the first century (possibly as far back as the first century B.C.E.) and the preserved writings of the authors of the Priestly Code and other Priestly writings of the Pentateuch of the sixth and fifth centuries B.C.E.

The Mishnah as we know it originated in its Division of Purities. The striking fact is that the Sixth Division is the only Division dating from before the wars that yields a complete and whole statement of a topic and its principal parts: (1) what imparts uncleanness; (2) which kinds of objects and substances may be unclean; and (3) how these objects or substances may regain the status of cleanness. Joined to episodic rulings elsewhere, the principal parts of the Sixth Division speak in particular of cleanness of meals, food and drink, pots and pans. It then would appear that the ideas ultimately expressed in the Mishnah began among people who had a special interest in observing cultic cleanness. There can be no doubt, moreover, that the context for such cleanness is the home, not solely the Temple. The issues of the law leave no doubt on that score. Since priests ate offerings at home and did so in a state of cleanness, it was a small step to apply the same taboos to food which was not a consecrated gift to the priests.

What is said through the keeping of these laws is that the food eaten at home, not deriving from the altar and its provision for the priesthood of meat not burned up in the fire, was as holy as the meal offerings, meat offerings, and drink offerings consecrated by being set aside for the altar and then in due course partly given to the priests and partly tossed on the altar and burned up. If food not consecrated for the altar, not protected in a state of cleanness (in the case of wheat), or carefully inspected for blemishes (in the case of beasts), and not eaten by priests in the Temple was deemed subject to the same restrictions as food consecrated for the altar, this carries implications about the character of that food, those who were to eat it, and the conditions in which it was grown. First, all food, not only that for the altar, was to be protected in a state of holiness, that is, separateness. Second, the place, the Land, in which the food was grown and kept was holy just like the Temple. Third, the people, Israel, who were to eat that food were holy just like the priesthood, in rank behind the Temple's chief caste. Fourth, the act of eating food anywhere in the holy Land was analogous to the act of eating food in the Temple, by the altar.

All of these obvious inferences from the repertory of laws we are going to survey point to a profound conviction about the Land, people, produce, condition, and context of nourishment. The setting was holy. The actors were holy. And what specifically they did which had to be protected in holiness was eating. For when they ate their food at home, they ate it the way priests did in the Temple. And the way priests ate their food in the Temple, the cultic rules and conditions observed in that setting, was like the way God ate his food in the Temple. That is to say, God's food and locus of nourishment were to be protected from the same sources of danger and contamination, preserved in the same exalted condition of sanctification. So by acting, that is, eating, like God, Israel became like God: a pure and perfect incarnation on earth in the Land which was holy, of the model of heaven. Eating food was the critical act just as the Priestly authors of Leviticus and Numbers had maintained when they made laws governing slaughtering beasts and burning up their flesh, baking pancakes and cookies with and without olive oil and burning them on the altar, pressing grapes and making wine and pouring it out onto the altar. The nourishment of the Land—meat, grain, oil, and wine—was set before God and burned ("offered up") in conditions of perfect cultic antisepsis.

In context this antisepsis provided protection against things deemed the opposite of nourishment, the quintessence of death: corpse matter, people who looked like corpses (Leviticus 13), dead creeping things, blood when not flowing in the veins of the living such as menstrual blood (Leviticus 15), other sorts of flux (semen in men, nonmenstrual blood in women) which yield not life but its opposite, death. What these excrescences have in common, of course, is that they are ambivalent. Why? Because they may be one thing or the other. Blood in the living is the soul; blood not in the living is the soul of contamination. The corpse was once a living person, like God; the person with skin like a corpse's and who looks dead was once a person who looked alive; the flux of the *zab* (Leviticus 15) comes from the flaccid penis, which under the right circumstances—that is, properly erect—produces semen and makes life. What is at the margin between life and death and can go either way is what is the source of uncleanness. But as we shall see, that is insufficient. For the opposite, in the Priestly Code, of *unclean* is not only *clean*, but also *holy*. The antonym is not to be missed: death or life, unclean or holy.

So the cult is the point of struggle between the forces of life and nourishment and the forces of death and extinction: meat, grain, oil, and wine, against corpse matter, dead creeping things, blood in the wrong setting, semen in the wrong context, and the like. Then on the occasions when meat was eaten, mainly at the time of festivals or other moments at which sin offerings and peace offerings were made, people

who wished to live ate their meat and at all times ate the staples of
wine, oil, and bread, in a state of life and so generated life. They kept
their food and themselves away from the state of death as much as
possible. And this heightened reality pertained at home as much as in
the Temple. The Temple was the font of life, the bulwark against death.

In this statement of the convictions of the Priestly Code about the
metaphysical meaning of cultic cleanness and taboos relevant thereto,
we see why Israelites interested in rules about meals would have
thought such rules in particular to be important. It is hardly surprising,
once the meal became a focus of attention, that the other two categories of the law (which I believe yield principles or laws deriving from
the period before the wars) present precisely the same sorts of rules.
Laws on growing and preparing food will attract attention as soon as
people wish to speak about how meals are to be eaten. That accounts
for the obviously lively interest in the biblical taboos of agriculture.
Furthermore, since meals are acts of society, they call together a group.
Outside the family, the natural unit, such a group will be special, cultic.
If a group is going to get together it will be on a Sabbath or festival,
not on a workday. So laws governing the making of meals on those
appointed times will inevitably receive attention. Nor is it surprising
that insofar as there are any rules pertinent to the cult they will involve
those aspects of the cult which apply also outside of the cult, that is,
how a beast is slaughtered, rules governing the disposition of animals
of a special status (e.g., firstborn), and the like.

That the rules for meals pertain not to isolated families but to a
larger group is strongly suggested by the other area which evidently
was subjected to sustained attention before the wars. I mean laws
governing who may marry whom. The context of the sayings assigned
to the authorities before the wars is the life of a small group of people
defining its life apart from the larger Israelite society while maintaining
itself wholly within that society. Three points of ordinary life formed
the focus for concrete, social differentiation: food, sex, and marriage.
What people ate, how they conducted their sexual lives, and whom
they married or to whom they gave their children in marriage would
define the social parameters of their group. These facts indicate who
was kept within the bounds and who was excluded and systematically
maintained at a distance. For these are the things—the only things—

subject to the independent control of the small group. The people behind the laws, after all, could not tell people other than their associates what to eat or whom to marry. But they could make their own decisions on these important matters. By making those decisions in one way and not in some other, moreover, they could keep outsiders at a distance and those who initially adhered to the group within bounds. Without political control they could not govern the transfer of property or other matters of public interest. But without political power they could and did govern the transfer of their women. It was in that intimate aspect of life that they thereby firmly established the outer boundary of their collective existence. The very existence of the group comes under discussion in the transfer of women. For that is the point at which the stress on order comes to expression, the strong interest in sanctification as a dimension of a well-ordered society and family.

That brings us to the Division of Appointed Times, which raises a different consideration to discuss the same principle, namely, sanctification of the everyday. The usable materials from before the wars in the Division of Appointed Times focus upon one significant issue: the preparation of meals on the festival day. To understand the rules dealing with meal preparation for festival days, we must recall the scriptural rule stated with special reference to the opening and closing festival days of Passover, that while one must not work on the festival, just as on the Sabbath one must not work, on the festival one may prepare a meal. This act of cooking, by contrast, may not be done on the Sabbath. Exod. 12:16 states the matter as follows: "On the first day you shall hold a holy assembly, and on the seventh day a holy assembly; no work shall be done on those days; but what every one must eat, that only may be prepared by you." The implications and application of this rule occupy all the usable rulings before 70, all of them assigned to the Houses by the redactors of the Mishnah, in the Division of Appointed Times.

We turn first to an explanation of how this particular set of problems most likely emerged from Scripture's rule. An egg laid on the festival day may be eaten that day, so the House of Shammai. The House of Hillel: it may not be eaten (*m. Bes.* 1:1–2; cf. *m. Bes.* 1:3–9; 2:1–5). At issue in this puzzling and bizarre dispute between the Houses of

Shammai and Hillel are the fundamental principles governing the preparation of meals on a festival day. As we just saw, Exod. 12:16 is clear that one may prepare food on the holy day. In this regard alone the holy day differs from the Sabbath on which one may not prepare food. Now the generative question, on which the Houses are made by the Mishnah redactors to take up all possible positions in diverse pericopes, is whether the festival day is the same as the Sabbath except in this one regard. The implication is that if so then every effort is to be made to differentiate actions of food preparation permitted on that day from equivalent actions on an ordinary day. If not, that is, if the festival is different from the Sabbath and so comparable to a weekday, then there is no reason on the festival to differentiate the mode of doing an action connected with preparation of food from the mode of doing so on an ordinary day; so the egg laid on the day may be eaten that day.

Another expression of this difference in principle is whether or not one must do in advance of the holy day all actions which need not be done on that day itself. If we invoke the analogy of the Sabbath then all actions that need not be done on the holy day must be done in advance. If we invoke the analogy of an ordinary secular day, then actions that need not be done on the festival day nonetheless may be done on that day. Now in the concrete disputes between the Houses, the two possible positions are attributed to them. What is important is raising the question. The most lenient position will be that by virtue of one's being permitted to prepare food on the festival day one also may do all actions, however remotely related, which are pertinent to the preparation of food. In the classic formulation one House prohibits doing acts only secondarily connected with food preparation, while the other permits one even to transport objects not used in cooking because one may transport objects that are used in cooking—thus the two most extreme positions.

The House of Shammai says that on a festival day people bring peace offerings (which yield food) but do not lay hands on them and they do not bring whole offerings (which yield no food for the sacrifice) at all. The House of Hillel maintains that they may bring both and lay hands on them (*m. Bes.* 2:4–5; cf. *m. Hag.* 1:2; 2:2). The consideration here again is the familiar one that one may prepare food on the festival day. At issue are actions indirectly related to cooking or not related at all. The Shammaites are represented as allowing the sacrifice of peace offerings from which the sacrificer—beneficiary of the rite—derives a good meat meal. But in that regard one need not lay hands on the beast. So that part of the rite is suspended. Whole offerings which are completely burned up are not offered at all. The House of Hillel now takes up the most lenient possible position permitting all actions of a given category because one of them is allowed, namely, the peace offerings which yield food.

The House of Shammai says: They take up bones and shells from the table (on the Sabbath). The House of Hillel says: One removes the entire table and shakes it out (*m. Shab.* 8:3). Since removing the bones and shells is incidental to the eating of the meal and obviously *is* permitted on the Sabbath, one may also handle those things which when not incidental to a meal serve no licit purpose and may not be handled on the Sabbath. The basic notion is that what serves a licit purpose is permitted, and what may not be used also may not be handled or touched. Subject to dispute now is whether one may handle what has served a permitted purpose but is no longer needed for said purpose, a refinement. The Shammaites here allow the person to continue to do so; the Hillelites allow only handling the table which in any event is allowed.

On a festival day which coincides with a Friday one may not cook for the following Sabbath day. But one may prepare food for the festival day itself and leave some over for use on the Sabbath. One also may prepare food on Thursday and add to that food on Friday, using on the Sabbath day what is left over on that account. The Houses differ on a trivial detail: how many different dishes are to be prepared in that regard (*m. Bes.* 2:1–3). The Sabbath and the festival day are two distinct and separate moments of sanctification. One may not do an act of labor—cooking, which is permitted on the festival—for purposes extrinsic to the observance of that festival. With that basic conception in mind this rule for "commingling of dishes" is not difficult to grasp. One may undertake food preparation in advance of both the festival and the following Sabbath, then continue that ongoing process through the festival with the result that food is left over for the Sabbath.

If we now stand back from the several cases and principles before us, we see that all take up a single problem, namely, the formation of principles and rules for preparing a meal on a special day. That day, the festival, is like the Sabbath in one way and it is not like the Sabbath in another. Consequently the generative issue is whether we spin out rules by analogy to the laws governing the Sabbath in the theory that the festival day is like the Sabbath, or in the theory that the festival is not like the Sabbath. In this latter case we shall have to find the outer limits of the contrastive laws. In sum, therefore, the specific problems investigated in the discrete pericopes pursue a single line of thought, namely, the contrastive-analogical model of pursuing the implications of a scriptural statement. That is, something is like something else and therefore follows the same rule or it is unlike something else and therefore follows the diametrically opposite rule. The fact is evident in the following sequence of propositions:

Scripture: One may prepare food on the festival day.

Houses: (1) One may do only what is directly connected with preparing food, *or* one may do even indirectly relevant actions.

(2) What is to be used on the festival must, *or* need not, be made ready for that purpose beforehand.

(3) What one does by permission on the festival must be done in a way different from an ordinary day, *or* one does such deeds in the normal way.

All three propositions naturally emerge as soon as one undertakes to compile rules to amplify and apply the scriptural law. (1) and (3) are complementary, in both instances simply seeking to define the limits of scriptural leniency. What (2) does is equally clear. Here is applied to the permissible activities of the festival precisely the consideration deemed urgent in connection with permissible actions and activities of the Sabbath. Just as in advance of the Sabbath one must designate an object which one plans to utilize on the Sabbath, so one must do the same in regard to a festival, now with respect to food that one may cook.

In sum, at issue in the entries in the names of the Houses before 70 are secondary questions generated by the intention to analyze and apply what Scripture permits. The basic conceptions are first, that the festival is analogous to the Sabbath in all regards except for the specified one and second, that what one is permitted to do on the festival is itself subject to qualification. In summary, rules in the Division of Appointed Times in fact deal with preparing meals, in this context, on the occasion of festivals. But the focus of interest is meals and the advent of the issue of the festival merely precipitates an inquiry into what in the case of the festival we have to say about making food.

It would appear that if someone had set out to organize a "Mishnah" before 70 the single operative category would have been making meals. He would have had a tractate on growing food in accord with certain biblical taboos and another on preparing food on the festival.

The laws in the Division of Purities pertinent to the age before the wars differ in one important way. While the other Divisions yield materials of an essentially random and episodic character, the Division of Purities presents us with laws which in the aggregate not only impart information but also tell a simple, whole story. That is, they form a complete system and it is the one which persists into the final version of the Mishnah. The topic, Purities, is treated in a particular way for a distinctive purpose. The story is about (1) how a source of uncleanness imparts uncleanness; (2) what sorts of objects are susceptible to uncleanness to begin with; and (3) how an unclean object may undergo a process of decontamination so as to return to its prior state of cleanness. What is important here is that the ultimate shape of the Division of Purities, as it will emerge in its final form in the Mishnah, is adumbrated by the materials before us, in primitive state and lacking detail, to be sure. These laws identify (1) sources of uncleanness; (2) principles definitive of objects which are susceptible to uncleanness (in addition to food and drink); and (3) modes of purification from uncleanness. The sources of uncleanness are those specified by Scripture. The Mishnah is able to add only substances analogous to the sources of uncleanness listed in Leviticus 12—15, Numbers 19, and other relevant passages. Scripture knows that food and drink, clothing and furniture may be made unclean. The Mishnah provides criteria for distinguishing those sorts of objects which are susceptible from those which are not susceptible to uncleanness. Finally, what restores the cleanness of an object made unclean is the action of water in its natural state. The Mishnah's founders speak of water unaffected by human intervention. Only water which has collected naturally and not been drawn in utensils or brought into a pool is suitable to restore the natural condition of what has been affected by the designated sources of uncleanness. While the second and third stages in the unfolding of the law will greatly expand and complicate these simple principles, the system ultimately revealed in the closed document already is before us in these three formative and definitive categories of interest and in the principles which shape the concrete rules operative in the several categories.

The earliest stage in the unfolding of the law of Purities deals with domestic matters, not cultic ones. The points of special concern begin with the uncleanness of a woman in her menstrual period, at which point she may not prepare food which is to be kept in a state of cultic cleanness or even sit on a chair and eat at a table at which a meal in a state of cultic cleanness is to be served. This matter brings us to the household and its hearth. The extensive early discourse of tractate Kelim on utensils susceptible to uncleanness is directed principally at domestic objects used for sleeping and eating. The principles of the tractate on immersion pools concern the restoration to cleanness of objects used in the home, exclusive of food and drink which are beyond purification. These are the points to which much intellectual energy would later be drawn. They are what would remain fresh and interesting in the law. The expansion of the sources of uncleanness rapidly reached limits imposed by the analogy utilized for that process. The contaminating power of corpse matter, like that of a corpse, leads nowhere beyond the simple allegation that what is like a corpse contaminates like a corpse. But when we come to the definition of what is susceptible to uncleanness on the one side, and what has the power to remove uncleanness on the other, we shall see much work done in the future.

It is no accident that those strata of Mishnaic law which appear to go back to the period before the wars deal specifically with the special laws of marriage (in Yebamot), distinctive rules on when sexual relations may and may not take place (in Niddah), and the laws covering the definition of sources of uncleanness and the attainment of cleanness, with specific reference to domestic meals (in certain parts of Oholot, Zabim, Kelim, and Miqvaot). Nor is it surprising that for the conduct of the cult and the sacrificial system, about which the group may have had its own doctrines but over which it neither exercised control nor even aspired to exercise control, there appears to be no systemic content or development whatsoever.

Once the group takes shape around some distinctive public issue or doctrine, as in odd taboos about eating, it also must take up the modes of social differentiation that will ensure the group's continued existence. For the group, once it comes into being, has to aspire to define and shape the ordinary lives of its adherents and to form a community expressive of its larger worldview. The foundations of an enduring community will then be laid down through rules governing what food may be eaten, under what circumstances, and with what sort of people; whom one may marry and what families may be joined in marriage; and how sexual relationships are to be timed, for example, in relationship to a woman's menstrual cycle. The Mishnah before the wars begins its life among a group of people who are joined together by a common conviction about the eating of food under ordinary circumstances in accord with cultic rules initially applicable, in the mind of the priestly lawyers of Leviticus and Numbers, to the Temple alone. This group, moreover, had other rules which affected who might join and who might not. As previously stated, these laws formed a protective boundary, keeping in those who were in, keeping out those who were not.

Why should the Temple and the ideas of its priests have played so important a role in the mind of the people who are represented by the earliest layer of ideas ultimately contained in the Mishnah? Since much of what the Mishnah presents is nothing other than what Scripture says, and since the Scriptures chosen for representation time and again are those in the Priestly Code, we have to wonder why the Priestly themes and repertoire of concerns should have so occupied the imagination and fantasy of the people who formed the group (or groups) represented in the laws before us. It is the continuity from the Priestly Code of the seventh through the fifth century B.C.E. to the beginnings of the Mishnaic code of the first and second centuries C.E. that requires explanation. For the Mishnah is the formation of the Priestly perspective on the condition of Israel.

The Mishnah states what priests had long said, but in other language and in other documents. True, the Mishnah has its own perspective and method. These are drastically different from those of the Priestly Code. The Mishnah employs the list-making method of the scribes. Indeed, the Mishnah takes up a remarkably unfriendly position on the priesthood, while acknowledging and affirming every single right and benefit owing to the priesthood. So, in sum, the Mishnah is not a merely contingent and secondary development of what is in the Priestly Code. Nonetheless, the continuity from the Priestly Code to the Mishnah is firm and impressive. If the founders of the Mishnaic code had something distinctive to say, it was in the vocabulary and images of the Priestly Code. The words were their own. But the deep syntax of the sacred, the metaphysical grammar, belonged to the priesthood from olden times. That is why it now becomes urgent to speculate on why the Priestly Code should have exercised so profound and formative an influence upon the founders and first framers of Mishnaic law.

How shall we account for the striking continuity from the Priestly Code to the Mishnah? The mode of answering the question is to point to the congruence between people's ideas and their social circumstance. The remarkable relevance to be discerned between Israel's abstract problems of thought and Israel's material situation is the center of the interpretive exercise.

The continuity from the Priestly writers to those of the Mishnah is clear. In theme and focus the Mishnah is mainly, though not solely, a Priestly document. That is why, to begin with, the Mishnah's principal themes and motifs, borrowed from the work of people of a much earlier age, have to be placed into continuity with the Priestly Code.

The Mishnah presents a way of organizing the world which only the priestly and other Temple castes and professions could have imagined. To point to obvious traits, we note that the document begins in its First Division with the claim that God owns the Land. The Land, therefore, must be used in a way consonant with the Land's holiness. More important, what the Land yields must be treated as belonging to God until the claims of God, the landlord, have been satisfied. These claims require that the calendar of the soil be set by the conduct of the cult in Jerusalem on the one side, and that the produce of the Land be set aside for the support of the cultic castes, priests, Levites, and their dependents on the other. The document proceeds to specify the appointed times of the year which are out of the ordinary. It does this by focusing upon two matters. First, the relevant appointed times are treated solely in terms of what is done in the cult in celebration of those special days. Second, rules governing conduct on appointed times in the towns and villages are so shaped as to bring the village and the Temple into a single continuum of sanctification. These are made into mirror images and complements of one another so that what may be done in the Temple may not be done in the village and vice versa. Just as the Temple is surrounded by its boundary, so the advent of the holy day causes the raising on the perimeters of the village of an invisible wall of sanctification as well. Two further principal divisions of the Mishnaic system take up the matter of the conduct of the cult on ordinary days (Holy Things) and the protection of the cult from dangerous forces, understood by the Mishnaic philosophers as forces of disruption and death (Purities). Uncleanness, which above all endangers the cult and must be kept away from the Temple, is what characterizes all lands but the holy Land. The lands of the Gentiles are unclean with corpse uncleanness. So death lies outside the holy Land, and life lies within the holy Land with its locus and apogee in the Temple and at the cult.

These statements ultimately made in the final versions of four of the six Divisions of the Mishnah would not have surprised the framers of the Priestly Code. Indeed, as we analyze the substantive character of the Mishnaic laws by their tractates, we find time and again that they constitute important statements not only *upon* Scripture, but also *of* what Scripture already has said. The tendency of the later Mishnaic thinkers is to amplify the principles they find in the Priestly Code, even while these same thinkers make an original and remarkably fresh statement upon what is in the Priestly Code. So, in sum, there is a close continuity at the deepest layers of sentiment and opinion between the Priestly Code and the Mishnah. Why is it that the framers of the Mishnah chose just these cultic and priestly matters for their painstaking and detailed study? Two significant factors come into play. First, we again take account of the beginnings of the Mishnaic system. Second, we rehearse what we have already said about the fundamental ecological facts which to begin with are confronted by the Priestly system, and which in later times, down to the closure of the Mishnah, remained definitive of the situation of Israel.

The Mishnaic system originates in the century or so before 70 among either lay people who pretended to be priests, or priests who took so seriously the laws governing their cultic activity that they concluded these same laws applied even outside the cult, or both (as in the Essene community of Qumran). When we reach the earliest possible suppositions of the earliest laws of Purities in particular, the givens of discourse turn out to maintain a closely related set of positions. As we just saw, cleanness, with special reference to food and drink, pots and pans, is possible outside the cult. Then cleanness is required outside of the cult. Also the cultic taboos governing the protection and disposition of parts of the sacrificial meat which are to be given to the priests apply to other sorts of food as well. They apply specifically to ordinary food, not food deriving from or related to the altar. The levitical taboos on sources of uncleanness therefore apply to ordinary food and, it follows, one must be careful to avoid these sources of uncleanness, or to undergo a rite of purification if one has had contact with said contaminating sources. Finally, the direction and purpose of the system as a whole in its earliest formulation are clearly to preserve the cleanness of the people of Israel, of the produce of the Land of Israel, of the sexual life of Israel, of the hearth and home of Israel. So the beginnings of the Mishnaic system lie among lay people pretending to be priests by eating their food at home as if they were priests in the Temple and also among priests with so intense a sense for cultic cleanness that they do the same. In sum, at the foundations were people who wished to act at home as if they were in the Temple, or to pretend that they must keep purity laws at home because their home and its life lay within the enchanted circle of the cult.

This position, invoking the cultic taboos for the Israelite home and table, in fact brings to fulfillment that Priestly position outlined in the Priestly Code. The social and cultural continuity of the Priestly perspective from Scripture to the Mishnah is illustrated when its founders maintain, as they do, that the cultic laws of Leviticus govern the Israelite table at home as much as the altar in the Temple of Jerusalem. I want to dwell on this matter with special reference to what is taken to be a principal and generative rule: the taboos about the menstruating woman's uncleanness.

When someone has in mind the problematic of purity at home and opens Scripture, attention is drawn to the conception that cleanness in respect to unclean bodily discharges must be kept so that the tabernacle will be clean: "Thus you shall keep the people of Israel separate from their uncleanness, lest they die in their uncleanness by defiling my tabernacle that is in their midst" (Lev. 15:31). But the menstruant, *zab*, *zabah*, and woman after childbirth do not go to the Temple. The Priestly Code is explicit that a rite of purification must be undertaken by the last three named (Lev. 15:13–15 for the *zab*, Lev. 15:28–30 for the *zabah*, and Lev. 12:6–8 for the woman after childbirth). Someone reading the Scripture will have asked, how are the unclean people going to make the Temple unclean when, in point of fact, before they are able to enter its precincts they undergo the rite of purification Scripture itself specifies? And the answer is that the people of Israel itself, *in whose midst is the tabernacle*, are to be kept clean so that the tabernacle, which is in their midst, will be in a clean setting. It will follow that the rules of cleanness in general pertaining to the Temple must apply as well to the people outside the Temple.

The rules of menstrual uncleanness and comparable uncleanness originally (before the revision accomplished by the Priestly redactors in the sixth or fifth century) had nothing to do with the cult. Menstrual taboos are not associated with the cult even in the very pericopes of the Priestly Code which refer to them. It is only in the subscription (Lev. 15:31) that the Priestly Code naturally insists upon an integral relationship between menstrual taboos and the cult and this, as stated earlier is even redactionally claimed only after the fact. We assume that men avoided having sexual relations with menstruating women without regard to whether or not a trip to the Temple was planned. Indeed, whether or not he even lived in the Land of Israel this taboo was presumably observed. Land, people, Temple—all form an integrated realm of being to be kept clean so as to serve as the locus of the sacred. Israel must be clean because of the tabernacle in their midst. Because the tabernacle is in their midst, Israel must be clean even when not in the tabernacle, which is exactly what Lev. 15:31 says—to someone who thought so to begin with.

The exclusiveness which constituted the response of priests and the followers of Ezra and Nehemiah to the critical problems of Israelite self-definition in the sixth and fifth centuries remained a pressing problem for the next six or seven hundred years because of continuing political and social changes. When we find that a formative group in Israelite society retained the fundamental perspectives and even the detailed laws which took shape to make a statement upon the definition of Israel in that one situation, we are on solid ground in asking whether the reason may be that the situation remained essentially the same. The perennial dilemmas endured fundamentally unchanged long afterward. Obviously, much that was new entered the Israelite social and political framework. Yet what we are constrained to call "Hellenization," meaning an epoch of internationalization and open borders, a cosmopolitan age of swiftly flowing currents in culture and thought, an era in which a common cosmopolitan culture spread throughout the great empire of the Mediterranean basin, expressed, to be sure, in an idiom distinctive to one group or some other—that "Hellenization" (preferably: *modernization*) remained a fact of life.

For from the moment at which trade and commerce in goods and ideas broke down walls of isolation of one group from another, one region from another, the issue of who each group was and what each group might claim for its own self-definition in order to explain its distinctive existence proved pressing. What was needed now were walls of another sort. No one now had to ask about what one group shared in common with all others. That was no issue. The answers in the cosmopolitan culture and economy were obvious. In the special case of Israel in the Land of Israel, moreover, there was a further issue. The dispersion among gentiles within the holy Land, the absence of contiguous settlement, the constant confrontation with other languages and other ways of life along with the preposterous claims of Scripture that Israel alone owned the Land, and Israel's God alone owned the world—these dissonances between social reality and imaginative fantasy raised to a point of acute concern what was in other settings a merely chronic and ongoing perplexity.

When we ask why the Temple with its cult proved enduringly central in the imagination of the Israelites in the country, as indeed it was, we have only to repeat the statements which the priests of the Temple and their imitators in the sects were prepared to make. These explain the critical importance of cult and rite. The altar was the center of life, the conduit of life from heaven to earth and from earth to heaven. All things are to be arrayed in relationship to the altar. The movement of the heavens demarcated and celebrated at the cult delineated the divisions of time in relationship to the altar. The spatial dimension of the Land was likewise demarcated and celebrated in relationship to the altar. The natural life of Israel's fields and corrals, the social life of its hierarchical caste-system, the political life (this was not only in theory by any means) centered on the Temple as the locus of ongoing government—all things in order and in place expressed the single message. The natural order of the world corresponded to, reinforced, and was reinforced by the social order of Israel. Both were fully realized in the cult, the nexus between those opposite and corresponding forces, the heavens and the earth.

The lines of structure emanated from the altar, and it was these lines of structure that constituted the high and impenetrable frontiers to separate Israel from the gentiles. Israel, which was holy, ate holy food, reproduced itself in accord with the laws of holiness, and conducted all of its affairs, both affairs of state and the business of the table and the bed, in accord with the demands of holiness. So the cult defined holiness. Holiness meant separateness. Separateness meant life. Why? Because outside of the Land, the realm of the holy, lay the domain of death. The lands are unclean. The Land is holy and so I stress that for the scriptural vocabulary one antonym for *holy* is *unclean*. The synonym of *holy* is *life*. The principal force and symbol of uncleanness and its highest expression is death. That is why cult plays so critical a role in the self-definition of Israel. Both the Priestly and Holiness Codes and the Mishnah in its beginnings express what makes Israel distinctive. Their shared message is one of metaphysics. But it can be stated as a judgment upon society as well: if the people are to live, it must be as a holy people. Imitating the holy God it must be wholly other, wholly different, set apart from the unclean lands of death on earth, just as God is set apart from the no-gods in heaven.

3

The Doctrine of Emotions and Its Long-term Uniformity in the Canonical History of Judaism's Ideas

The doctrine of emotions in the view of the sages who created Judaism remained always the same. The reason derives from the social realities that give meaning to emotion and definition to the possibilities of feeling. If we begin with feeling, we end up in society. Why? Because affections constitute a construct of culture. A small step takes us to the position that affections no less than convictions signify something beyond themselves. So emotions should be interpreted as forms of symbolic behavior. The heart's deep sentiments serve as symbols and therefore affectively speak a social vocabulary.

How I feel stands for everyone all at once. In the language of theology of the Judaism of a later age the *Mensch* of the Yiddish language, the fully human person, must become the Israel-*Mensch*. And who is this? It is the Judaic human being harmonious in affection, action, and affirmation. Together these determine who is Israel, the Jewish nation—one by one and all together.

In the Western Protestant tradition of Edwards and Schleiermacher we take it for granted that emotions speak for the private individual, not for the nation. In the tradition of philosophy from the Greeks onward, moreover, emotions speak not rationally but irrationally. This other view, that of the ancient sages (a view that is also gaining currency in contemporary philosophy and psychology), sees the matter differently. It regards emotions as artifacts of culture and conceives

51

that emotions lay down judgments. They therefore emerge as rational, public, and social, speaking not only for the individual but also to him or her. Feelings, too, define modes of symbolic behavior, as noted. When we examine the doctrine of emotions in the canonical writings of formative Judaism, we enter a world to which it is self-evident that feeling is subject to law and emotion is a matter of lesson and tradition.

The canonical writings from the Mishnah through the Talmud of Babylonia lay down a set of rules about the affective life. Emotions, as much as deeds on the one side, and convictions or opinions or deliberations on the other, constitute a category of the religious life. One may sin by feeling as much as by action or affirmation. One may serve God in the heart—and in the heart alone without regard to conviction or action—as much as in the mind and in the life of doing what is commanded and not doing what is forbidden. The doctrine of emotions remains remarkably stable from the beginning to the end of the canonical history of Judaism in its formative age.

In many categories of thought we cannot reasonably define what "Judaism," or "our sages," thought all at once and all together. Why not? Because the components of the canonical literature of Judaism, arrayed in sequence of closure, yield ample evidence of change, development, growth, above all response to circumstance and context. But here the sources read sequentially do not. So while the formative centuries of the history of Judaism mark a period of remarkable growth and change with history consisting of sequences of developments in various substantial ideas and generative conceptions, here in the matter of emotions it does not. The single fact emerging from a survey of the canon read in the order at hand is that the sages' doctrine of affections remained a constant.

Before we inquire further about that fact, let us rapidly review the main points established in a probe of the main canonical compositions from the Mishnah through the Bavli and the more important compilations of biblical exegeses.

While the authorship of the Mishnah casually refers to emotions—for example, tear of joy, tears of sorrow—it always is in a public and communal context. Where there is an occasion of rejoicing, one form of joy is not to be confused with some other, or one context with another. Accordingly, marriages are not to be held on festivals (*m.*

M.Q. 1:7). Likewise, mourning is not to take place (*m. M.Q.* 1:7). Where emotions play a role it is because of the affairs of the community at large, as in rejoicing on a festival, mourning on a fast day (*m. Suk.* 5:1–4). Emotions are to be kept in hand, as in the case of the relatives of the executed felon (*m. San.* 6:6). The single underlying principle affecting all forms of emotions for the Mishnah is that feelings must be kept under control, never fully expressed without reasoning about the appropriate context. Emotions must always lay down judgments. We see in most of those cases in which emotions play a systemic and not merely tangential role, that the basic principle is the same. We can and must so frame our feelings as to accord with the appropriate rule. In only one case does emotion play a decisive role in settling an issue, and that has to do with whether or not a farmer was happy that water came upon his produce or grain. That case underlines the conclusion just now drawn. If people feel a given sentiment, it is a matter of judgment and therefore invokes the law's penalties. So in this system emotions are not treated as spontaneous but as significant aspects of a person's judgment. It would be difficult to find a more striking example of that view than at *m. Makh.* 4:5 and related passages. The very fact that the law applies comes about because the framers judge the farmer's feelings to constitute, on their own and without associated actions or even conceptions, final and decisive judgments on what has happened.

Tractate Abot presents the single most comprehensive account of religious affections. The reason is that in that document above all, how we feel defines a critical aspect of virtue. The issue proves central, not peripheral. The doctrine emerges fully exposed. A simple catalogue of permissible feelings comprises humility, generosity, self-abnegation, love, a spirit of conciliation of the other, and eagerness to please. A list of impermissible emotions is made up of envy, ambition, jealousy, arrogance, sticking to one's opinion, self-centeredness, a grudging spirit, vengefulness, and the like. People should aim at eliciting from others acceptance and good will and should avoid confrontation, rejection, and humiliation of the other. This they do through conciliation and giving up their own claims and rights. So both catalogues form a harmonious and uniform whole, aiming at the cultivation of the humble and malleable person, one who accepts everything and resents nothing.

True, these virtues, in this tractate as in the system as a whole, count—which is what God wants. But God favors those who please others. The virtues appreciated by human beings prove identical to the ones to which God responds as well. The virtues of the heart that encompass the rest are restraint (the source of self-abnegation) and humility (the antidote for ambition, vengefulness, and above all, arrogance). It is restraint of our own interest that enables us to deal generously with others and humility about ourselves that generates a liberal spirit towards others.

So the emotions prescribed in tractate Abot turn out to provide variations of a single feeling, which is the sentiment of the disciplined heart, whatever affective form it may take. And where does the heart learn its lessons, if not in relationship to God? So: "Make his wishes yours, so that he will make your wishes his" (Abot 2:4). Applied to the relationships between human beings, this inner discipline of the emotional life will yield exactly those virtues that the framers of tractate Abot spell out in one example after another. Imputing to heaven exactly those responses felt on earth—"Anyone from whom people take pleasure, God takes pleasure" (Abot 3:10)—makes the point at the most general level.

When the authors or compilers of the Tòsefta finished their labor of amplification and complement, they had succeeded in adding only a few important developments of established themes. What is striking is first, the stress upon the communal stake in an individual's emotional life. Still more striking is the Tosefta's authors' explicit effort to invoke an exact correspondence between public and private feelings. In both realms emotions are to be tamed, kept in hand and within accepted proportions. Public sanctions for inappropriate or disproportionate emotions entail emotions, for instance, shame. It need hardly be added that feeling shame for improper feelings once again underlines the social, judgmental character of those feelings. People are responsible for how they feel, as much as for how in work or deed they express feeling. Hence an appropriate penalty derives from the same aspect of social life, that is, the affective life.

There is no more stunning tribute to the power of feeling than the allegation, first surfacing in the Tosefta, that the Temple was destroyed because of vain hatred. That sort of hatred, characterized as self-serving and arrogant, stands against the feelings of love that characterize God's relationship to Israel. Accordingly, it was improper affections that destroyed this relationship embodied in the Temple cult of old. Given the critical importance accorded the Temple cult the sages could not have made more vivid their view that how a private person feels shapes the public destiny of the entire nation. So the issues came to expression in heightened stakes. But the basic position of the authors of the Mishnah, inclusive of their first apologists in Abot, seems entirely consistent. What Tosefta's authors accomplished is precisely what they claimed, which was to amplify, supplement, and complement established principles and positions.

The principal result of a survey of the present topic in the pages of the Yerushalmi will confirm our thesis. Emotions not taken up earlier did not now come under discussion. Principles introduced earlier enjoyed restatement and extensive exemplification and might even generate secondary developments of one kind or another. But nothing absent at the outset drew sustained attention later on. The system proved essentially complete in the earliest statement of its main points. Everything that followed for four hundred years served to reinforce and restate what had emerged loud and clear at the outset. What then do the authors or compilers of the Yerushalmi contribute? Temper marks the ignorant person, restraint and serenity the learned one. In general, we notice that where the Mishnah introduces into its system issues of the affective life the Yerushalmi's authors and compilers will take up those issues. But they rarely introduce them on their own and never say much new about those they treat. What we find is instruction to respect public opinion and cultivate social harmony.

What is most interesting in the Yerushalmi is the recognition that there are rules descriptive of feelings as much as of other facts of life. These rules tell us how to dispose of cases in which feelings make a difference. The fact is, therefore, that the effects of emotions as much as of opinions or deeds come within the rule of law. It must follow, in the view of the sages, that the affective life once more proves an aspect of society. People are assumed to frame emotions, as much as opinions, in line with common and shared judgments. In no way do emotions form a special classification expressive of what is private, spontaneous, individual, and beyond the law and reason.

The Bavli carried forward with little change the traditional program of emotions, listing the same ones catalogued earlier and no new ones. The authors said about those feelings what had been said earlier. A leader must be someone acceptable to the community. God then accepts him too. People should be ready to give up quarrels and forgive. The correspondence of social and personal virtues reaches explicit statement. How so? The community must forbear, the individual must forgive. Communal tolerance for causeless hatred destroyed the Temple; individual vendettas yield miscarriages. The two coincide. In both cases people nurture feelings that express arrogance. Arrogance is what permits the individual to express emotions without discipline, and arrogance is what leads the community to undertake what it cannot accomplish.

A fresh emphasis of the Bavli favored mourning and disapproved of rejoicing. We can hardly maintain that this view came to expression only in the latest stages in the formation of the canon. The contrary is the case. The point remains consistent throughout. Excessive levity marks arrogance, deep mourning characterizes humility. So many things come down to one thing. The nurture of an attitude of mourning should mark both the individual and the community, both in mourning for the Temple and in mourning for the condition of nature, including the human condition, signified by the Temple's destruction.

A mark of humility is humble acceptance of suffering. This carried forward Aqiba's view that present suffering produces future joy. The ruin of the Temple served as a guarantee that just as the prophetic warnings came to realization, so too would prophetic promises of restoration and redemption.

In the realm of feelings the union of opposites came about through the same mode of thought. Hence God's love comes to fulfillment in human suffering, and the person who joyfully accepts humiliation or suffering will enjoy the appropriate divine response of love. Another point at which the authors of the Bavli introduce a statement developing a familiar view derives from the interpretation of how to love one's neighbor. It is by imposing upon one's neighbor the norms of the community, rebuking the other for violating accepted practice. In

this way the emotion of love takes on concrete social value in rein-
forcing the norms of the community. Since the verse at hand invites
exactly that interpretation, we can hardly regard the Bavli's paragraph
on the subject as innovative. Stories about the sages rang the changes
on the themes of humility, resignation, restraint, and perpetual good
will. A boastful sage loses his wisdom. A humble one retains it. Since
it is wisdom about which a sage boasts, the matching of opposites
conforms to the familiar mode of thought.

The strikingly fresh medium for traditional doctrines in the Bavli
takes the form of prayers composed by the sages. Here the values of
the system came to eloquent expression. Sages prayed that their souls
may be as dust for everyone to tread upon. They asked for humility
in spirit, congenial colleagues, good will, and good impulses. They
asked God to take cognizance of their humiliation, to spare them
disgrace. The familiar affective virtues and sins, self-abnegation as
against arrogance, made their appearance in liturgical form as well.
Another noteworthy type of continuing material in which the pages
of the Bavli prove rich portrayed the deaths of the sages. One dominant
motif is uncertainty in the face of death, a sign of humility and self-
abnegation.

The basic motif—theological as much as affective—encompassing
all materials is evident. Israel is estranged from God, therefore should
exhibit the traits of humility and uncertainty, acceptance and conciliation. When God recognizes the proper feelings in Israel's heart, as
much as in the nation's deeds and deliberation, God will respond by
ending that estrangement that marks the present age. So the single
word encompassing the entire affective doctrine of the canon of Judaism is alienation. No modern analyst can miss the psychological
depth of the system which joins the human condition to the fate of
the nation and the world and links the whole to the heart of God. A
survey of compilations of exegeses of Scripture will make the same
point. There is nothing new, only ample restatement of everything
familiar.

We therefore find ourselves where we started in the Mishnah and
Abot, in those sayings that say if one wants something, he or she should
aspire to its opposite. Things are never what they seem. To be rich,
accept what you have. To be powerful, conciliate your enemy. To be

endowed with recognition in which to take pride, express humility. So too the doctrine of the emotional life expressed in law, scriptural interpretation, and tales of the sages alike turns out to be uniform. Emotions will end up uncontrolled and spontaneous. Anger, vengeance, pride, arrogance—these people feel by nature. So feelings as much as affirmations and actions must become what by nature they are not. If one wants riches, seek the opposite. If one wants honor, pursue the opposite. If Israel wants the Messiah, Israel must *do* nothing but *become* holy. How do you seek the opposite of wealth? It is by accepting what you have. And how pursue humility if not by doing nothing to aggrandize oneself? So the life of the emotions, in conformity to the life of reflection and of concrete deed (not to mention public policy and politics), will consist in the transformation of what things *seem* into what they *ought* to be. No contemporary psychologist or philosophy can fail to miss the point. Here we have an example of the view—whether validated by the facts of nature or not—that emotions constitute constructs and feelings form the basis of judgments. So the heart belongs, together with the mind, to the human being's powers to form reasoned viewpoints. Coming from the sages, intellectuals to their core, such an opinion surely coheres with the context and circumstance of those who hold it.

This theory of the emotional life, persistent through the unfolding of the canonical documents of Judaism, fits into a larger way of viewing the world. How shall we describe this mode of thought? We may call it an *as-if* way of seeing things. That is to say, it is *as if* a common object or symbol really represented an uncommon one. Nothing says what it means. All statements carry deeper meaning which inheres in other statements altogether. So too each emotion bears a negative and positive charge as each matches and balances the other: humility, arrogance; love, hate. If what is natural to the heart is a negative emotion then the individual has power to sanctify that negative, sinful feeling and turn it into a positive, holy emotion. Ambition must be tamed and so transformed into humility; hatred and vengeance must change into love and acceptance.

How shall we describe the program for feeling as much as for thought? What we see in the surveyed materials is an application of a large-scale, encompassing exercise in analogical thinking: something is like something else, stands for, evokes, or symbolizes that which is quite outside itself. It may be the opposite of something else, in which case it conforms to the exact opposite of the rules that govern that something else. The reasoning is analogical or it is contrastive, and the fundamental logic is taxonomic. The taxonomy rests on those comparisons and contrasts that are metonymic and parabolic. In that case what lies on the surface misleads. What lies beneath or beyond the surface is the true reality.

How shall we characterize people who see things this way? They have become accustomed to perceiving more—or less—than what is at hand. Perhaps that is a natural mode of thought for the Jews of this period (and not them alone), so long used to calling themselves God's first love, yet now seeing others with greater worldly reason claiming that same advantaged relationship. The radical disjuncture between the way things were and the way Scripture said things were supposed to be—and in actuality would someday become—surely imposed an unbearable tension. It was one thing for the slave born to slavery to endure. It was another for the free man sold into slavery to accept that same condition. The vanquished people, the broken-hearted nation that had lost its city and its Temple, that had even produced another nation from its midst to take over its Scripture and much else, could not bear too much reality. That defeated people (in its intellectuals as represented in the sources we have reviewed) found refuge in a mode of thought that trained vision to see things otherwise than as the eyes perceived them. Among the diverse ways by which the weak and subordinated accommodate to their circumstance, the one of iron-willed pretense in life is most likely to yield the mode of thought at hand: things never are, because they cannot be, what they seem. The uniform tradition on emotions persisted intact because the social realities of Israelite life remained constant.

If the reader concurs that emotions are portrayed in essentially one way throughout the formation of Judaism, then the obvious question must now come to center stage: so what? We may fairly ask why we should regard as a fact demanding explanation the simple observation that a single view of human nature, including permissible and forbidden feelings, predominates among a coherent social group of intellectuals. People take for granted, not entirely without reason, that the sages' culture defined itself along traditional lines. A mark of the disciple of the sage was imitation of the master. A critical doctrine of the Judaism defined by the sages of the rabbinical canon emphasized that people memorized the received books of rules and exegesis and made decisions (as in any tradition of jurisprudence) in line with those already made. A list of those definitive traits of the book-culture portrayed by the canon would encompass pages of items characteristic of a traditional, stable, uniform, and therefore constant culture. Why then should we have expressed an interest in demonstrating so unsurprising a fact as the constancy of the doctrine of emotions in the literary culture fully exposed in the sequence of writings we have surveyed?

The answer requires two sentences. First, in general, traditional cultures and even literary cultures do change over time, which in the present case covers a span of five hundred years. Second, we shall see three important examples of how, within the same canon and read in the same sequence, definitive traits of culture exhibit massive marks of revision. These examples are hermeneutics, symbolism, and teleology.

We therefore recognize that in the formation of Judaism some things changed, others remained constant. What changed? Fundamentals of Judaism, the generative exegetical method, the critical symbol, the teleological doctrine. What remained the same? The program of emotions, the sages' statement of how people should feel and why they should take charge of their emotions. The same books, read in the same order, which reveal the one in flux portray the other in stasis. No one can imagine that Jews in their hearts felt the way the sages said they should. The repertoire of permissible and forbidden feelings defined the broad range of actual emotions, whether private or social, of the community of Israel. In fact we have no evidence about how people really felt. We see only a picture of what the sages thought they should and should not feel.

But as has been stressed, the unchanging repertoire of feelings strikingly contrasts with the shifts and turns of critical components of Judaism as these emerge in the same authoritative writings. Writings that reveal stunning shifts in doctrine, teleology, and hermeneutical method lay forth from beginning to end the one picture of the ideal

Israelite. It is someone who accepts, forgives, conciliates, makes the soul like dirt beneath other people's feet.

Why the sages counseled a different kind of courage is obvious. Given the situation of Israel, vanquished on the battlefield, broken in the turnings of history's wheel, we need hardly wonder why wise men advised conciliation and acceptance. Exalting humility made sense, there being little choice. Whether or not these virtues found advocates in other contexts for other reasons, in the circumstance of the vanquished nation and for the people of broken heart, the policy of forbearance proved instrumental, entirely appropriate to both the politics and social condition at hand.

How so? If Israel produced a battlefield hero, the nation could not give him an army. If Jewry cultivated the strong-minded individual, it sentenced such a person to a useless life of ineffective protest. The nation required not strong-minded leadership but consensus. The social virtues of conciliation reinforced the bonds that joined the nation lacking frontiers, the people without a politics of its own. For all there was to hold Israel together to sustain its life as a society would have to come forth out of the sources of inner strength. Bonding emerged only from within. So consensus, conciliation, self-abnegation and humility defined appropriate emotions because they dictated wise policy and shrewd politics.

Israel could survive only on the sufferance of others. It therefore would nurture not merely policies of subordination and acceptance of diminished status among nations. Israel also would develop in its own heart the requisite emotional structure. The composition of individuals' hearts would then comprise the counterpart virtues. A policy of acceptance of the rule of others dictated affections of conciliation to the will of others. A defeated people meant to endure defeat would have to get along by going along. How to persuade each Jew to accept what all Jews had to do to endure? Persuade the heart, not only the mind. Then each one privately would feel what everyone publicly had in any case to think.

This state of affairs accounts for the persistence of the sages' wise teachings on temper, their sagacious counsel on conciliating others and seeking the approval of the group.

Let me close with a thesis in two parts. First, what endures lasts because society sets the terms of persistence. Second, what undergoes metamorphosis changes because the social group does not sustain that aspect of the given.

Persistence is of two orders. A single program of emotions defined how long generations of Israel, over many centuries, were supposed by the sages to live out the affective life. Expressions of a single basic mind-set (as expressed in the Priestly Code), achieved realization over time in diverse forms and social group. In one case, therefore, the details remained the same and nothing much changed. In the other, the fundamental worldview remained intact, while the way of life underwent substantial revision in accord with circumstance. The difference, of course, derives from the diversity of social groups at hand. In the case of our picture of the emotional life of Israel, a single ongoing group stands behind the entire corpus of evidence. In the instance of our knowledge of the persistence in diverse expressions of a single version of imagination and fantasy, what we know comes to us from two or three groups.

Change by contrast turns out to follow a single order. Where within a system we see marks of reformation (as we do when we take up method, symbolic system, and teleology of Judaism in its formative age), we perceive change because we have subjected to a close and analytical reading a canon that in composition spread over a long period of time. From a great distance the values appear uniform. Close up, they prove diverse. But change is not only in the eye of the beholder. The differences from phase to phase prove real and profound.

To understand change, we appeal to that same court to which we addressed our question about constancy: namely, the basic structure and construction of the social group. When symbols change, our attention is drawn to social change beyond. And when society changes, we ask how its symbolic system—expressed in ways of life and in worldview—has shifted. Each must come to testify to the condition of the other. So as a matter of hypothesis we must speculate about the interplay of society and symbol. The striking shifts in method, symbol of doctrine, and teleology revealed in the unfolding of the canon of Judaism in its formative changes point toward changes in the social world of Israel, as the sages, among all Israel, perceived that social context.

Why then the coincidence in the pages of the Yerushalmi in particular of change in three critical components of the symbolic structure
of the sages' Judaism? When we recall that the movement from the
Mishnah to the Yerushalmi for the third- and earlier fourth-century
writings follows a single path, the one laid out by the authorship of
the Mishnah, and then in the late fourth-century and subsequent documents takes an amazing turn, we realize the urgency of the question.
We turn to this matter next.

PART THREE

WHEN CHRISTIANITY
MADE
A DIFFERENCE

4

The Canonical History of Ideas in the Formative Age of Judaism

We have made passing reference several times to "the canonical history of ideas." Let us now explain this approach to the reading of the rabbinical writings of late antiquity, spelling out the sort of history that it does and does not yield.

The formative age of Judaism is the period marked at the outset by the Mishnah, taking shape from sometime before the Common Era and reaching closure at ca. 200 C.E., and at the end by the Talmud of Babylonia, ca. 600 C.E. In between these dates, two streams of writings developed, one legal, explaining the meaning of the Mishnah, the other theological and exegetical, interpreting the sense of Scripture. The high points of the former come with tractate Abot which is the Mishnah's first apologetic, then Tosefta, a collection of supplements ca. 300 C.E., the Talmud of the Land of Israel ca. 400 C.E., followed by the Babylonian Talmud. The latter set of writings comprise compositions on Exodus, in Mekilta attributed to R. Ishmael and of indeterminate date, Sifra on Leviticus, Sifre on Numbers, and another Sifre, on Deuteronomy at a guess to be dated at ca. 300 C.E., then Genesis Rabbah ca. 400 C.E., Leviticus Rabbah ca. 425 C.E., and at the end, Pesiqta de Rab Kahana, Lamentations Rabbati, and some other treatments of biblical books, all of them in the fifth or sixth centuries. These books and some minor related items together form the canon of Judaism as it had reached its definitive shape by the end of late antiquity.

If we lay out these writings in the approximate sequence in which
they reached closure beginning with the Mishnah, the Tosefta, then
Sifra and its associated compositions, followed by the Talmud of the
Land of Israel, and alongside Genesis Rabbah and Leviticus Rabbah,
then Pesiqta de Rab Kahana and its companions, and finally the Talmud of Babylonia, we gain what I call "canonical history." This is,
specifically, the order of the appearance of ideas when the documents,
read in the outlined sequence, address a given idea or topic. The consequent history consists of the sequence in which a given statement
on the topic at hand was made (early, middle, or late) in the unfolding
of the canonical writings.

To illustrate the process, what does the authorship of the Mishnah
have to say on the theme? Then how does the compositor of Abot
deal with it? Then the Tosefta's compositor's record comes into view,
followed by the materials assembled in the Talmud of the Land of
Israel, alongside those now found in the earlier and middle ranges of
compilations of scriptural exegeses, and as always, the Talmud of
Babylonia at the end.

In the three chapters that follow we shall read the sources in exactly
the order outlined here. I produce pictures of how these sources treat
three important principles of Judaism: hermeneutics, teleology, and
symbol. In each case we shall see important shifts and changes in the
unfolding of ideas on the principles under study. At the end it will
emerge that the turning point in all three instances comes with the
Talmud of the Land of Israel at ca. 400 C.E. Later, when we read the
same books in the same order and for the same purpose—the tracing
of canonical history—we shall note that what is said in the successive
documents on another critical issue remains remarkably uniform
throughout. The canonical history in that matter yields a story of
continuity and stability, not drastic change at a given point.

So, in sum, this story of continuity and change rests upon the notion
that we can present the history of the treatment of a topical program
in the canonical writings of that Judaism. I do not claim that the
documents represent the state of popular or synagogue opinion. I do
not know whether the history of the idea in the unfolding official texts
corresponds to the history of the idea among the people who stand
behind those documents. Even less do I claim to speak about the his-

tory of the topic or idea at hand outside of rabbinical circles, among the Jewish nation at large. All these larger dimensions of the matter lie wholly beyond the perspective of this book. The reason is that the evidence at hand is of a particular sort and hence permits us to investigate one category of questions and not another. The category is defined by established and universally held conventions about the order in which the canonical writings reached completion. Therefore we trace the way in which matters emerge in the sequence of writings followed here.

We trace the way in which ideas were taken up and spelled out in these successive stages in the formation of the canon. Let the purpose of the exercise be emphasized: *When we follow this procedure, we discover how, within the formation of the rabbinical canon of writings, the idea at hand came to literary expression and how it was then shaped to serve the larger purposes of the nascent canonical system as a whole.*

By knowing the place and uses of the topic under study within the literary evidences of the rabbinical system, we gain a better understanding of the formative history of that system. What do we not learn? Neither the condition of the people at large nor the full range and power of the rabbinical thinkers' imagination comes to the fore. About other larger historical and intellectual matters we have no direct knowledge at all. Consequently we claim to report only what we learn about the canonical literature of a system evidenced by a limited factual base. No one who wants to know the history of a given idea in all the diverse Judaisms in late antiquity, or the role of that idea in the history of all the Jews in all parts of the world in the first seven centuries of the Common Era will find it here.

In order to understand the method we must recognize the character of the evidence presented. The sources constitute a collective, and therefore official, literature. All of the documents took shape and attained a place in the canon of the rabbinical movement as a whole. None was written by an individual in such a way as to testify to personal choice or decision. Accordingly, we cannot provide an account of the theory of a given individual at a particular time and place. We have numerous references to what a given individual said about the topic at hand. But these references do not reach us in the authorship of that person, or even in his language. They come to us only in the setting of a *collection* of sayings and statements, some associated with names, other unattributed and anonymous. The collections by definition were composed under the auspices of rabbinical authority—a school or a circle. They tell us what a group of people wished to preserve and hand on as authoritative doctrine about the meaning of the Mishnah and Scripture. The compositions reach us because the larger rabbinical estate chose to copy and hand them on. Accordingly, we know the state of doctrine at the stages marked by the formation and closure of the several documents.

The alternative method is to assume that if a given document ascribes an opinion to a named authority the opinion actually was stated in that language by that sage. On this assumption a much richer history of an idea, not merely of the literary evidences of that idea, may be worked out without regard only to the date of the document at hand. Within this theory of evidence, we have the history of what individuals thought on a common topic.

It is obvious why we cannot proceed to outline the sequence of ideas solely on the basis of the sequence of the sages to whom ideas are attributed. We simply cannot demonstrate that a given authority really said what a document assigns to him. Let me list the range of uncertainty that necessitates this approach.

First, if the order of the documents were fully sound and the contents representative of rabbinical opinion, then the result would be a history of the advent of the idea at hand and the development and articulation of that idea in formative Judaism. We should then have a fairly reliable picture of ideas at hand as these unfolded in orderly sequence. But we do not know that the canonical history corresponds to the actual history of ideas. Furthermore, we cannot even be sure that the order of documents presently assumed in scholarly convention is correct.

Second, if a rabbi really spoke the words attributed to him, then a given idea would have reached expression within Judaism *prior* to the redaction of the document. Dividing things up by documents will tend to give a later date and thus a different context for interpretation to opinions held earlier than we can presently demonstrate.

Third, although we are focusing upon the literature produced by a particular group, again we have no clear notion of what people were thinking outside that group. We therefore do not know how opinions held by other groups or by the Jewish people in general came to shape the vision of rabbis. When, for example, we note that there also existed poetic literature and translations of Scriptures characteristic of the synagogue worship, we cannot determine whether the poetry and most translations spoke for rabbis or for some quite different group.

For these reasons I have chosen to address the contextual question within the narrow limits of the canon. Obviously, if I could in a given formulation relate the appearance of a given idea to events affecting rabbis in particular or to the life of Israel in general, the results would be exceedingly suggestive. But since we do not know for whom the documents speak, how broadly representative they are, or even how comprehensive is their evidence about rabbis' views, we must carefully define what we do and do not know. So for this early stage in research the context in which a given idea is described, analyzed, and interpreted is the canon. But this first step alone carries us to new territory. I hope that in due course others will move beyond the limits which, at the moment, seem to me to mark the farthest possible advance.

5

Change in the Symbolization of the Other: Rome from Place to Sibling

THE ISSUE OF METHOD

The relationships between Rome and Israel in late antiquity, from the destruction of the Temple in 70 C.E. to the Muslim conquest of the Land of Israel in the mid-seventh century, have attracted attention over the years.[1] What scholars have done, when approaching the rabbinic writings of the age, is to collect and organize all the sayings on Rome and to treat the resulting composite as "the talmudic," or "the rabbinic" view of Rome. In doing so they have followed the established method in which to investigate the thought of classical Judaism on any given subject. It is to collect pertinent sayings among the diverse documents and to assemble the all these sayings into a composite, a portrait, "*the* rabbinic view of Rome." The composite will divide up the sayings in accord with the logic of the topic at hand.

My research for a number of years has led me to differentiate among documents and to ask each document to deliver its particular viewpoint. When, therefore, I wish to trace the history of an idea, it produces the representations of that idea as yielded by documents, read singly and one by one, then in the sequence of their closure.[2] I do not

---

1. See, for the first systematic work, Shmuel Krauss, *Persia and Rome in Talmud and Midrash* (Jerusalem, 1947, in Hebrew).
2. For reasons I spell out in my *Religious Study of Judaism: Description, Analysis, Interpretation.* First Series (Atlanta: Scholars Press, 1985), I call this the "canonical history of ideas." See above, pp. 67–71.

73

join together everything I find, without regard to its point of origin
in a given compilation of rabbinic sayings. Rather I keep things apart,
so that I record what I find in document A, then in document B, and
onward through the alphabet. What this yields is a history of the idea
at hand as the documents, laid out in their sequence, reveal that
history.

Now how shall we test whether the approach just now outlined
proves superior to the established one? The answer is to ask what we
discover if we do not differentiate among documents, as against what
we find when we do. If differentiating yields results we should have
missed had we not read the documents one by one, then our category
has obscured important points of difference. If *not* differentiating
yields a unity that differentiating has obscured, so that the parts, seen
all together, appear to cohere, then the category that has required
differentiation has obscured important points in common.

Let us now proceed to review four important sources as autonomous
components of a larger canon and to ask each of them to speak for
itself on the topic at hand. These fall into two groups: the Mishnah
(inclusive of tractate Abot) and a document of Mishnah exegesis, the
Tosefta, and two documents of Scripture exegesis, Genesis Rabbah
and Leviticus Rabbah. The former testify to the minds of compositors
who flourished in the late second and third centuries (before Christianity became the state religion of the Roman Empire), the latter, the
late fourth and fifth centuries (after the establishment of Christianity
as imperial cult and faith). We shall parse the ideas at hand as they
unfold in these four compilations.[3] Then we shall trace the result,
which is the canonical history of the topic at hand. Finally, we shall
review the original results and show where and how they erred—and,

3. Since we cannot demonstrate that what is attributed to authorities within the pages
of these documents really was said by them, we also cannot impute to a generation
prior to that of redaction any of the ideas expressed in the several documents: what we
cannot show, we do not know. And, to the contrary, what we can show, which is that
the documents demonstrably speak for the authorship of the final redaction, we do
know: the opinions of the ultimate, sometimes also the penultimate, redactors. That is
all we know at this time. So whether or not the Mishnah or Leviticus Rabbah contains
ideas held prior to the generation of redaction is not at issue. I claim here to say what
the authorship at the end wished to state, in the time and circumstance of redaction.
What else these documents contain, to what other ages and authorships they testify—
these are separate questions, to be taken upon in their own terms.

above all, explain the reason why. In that way we shall carry out an exercise in the testing of a method. That is to say, we ask what happens when we differentiate and when we do not.

DIFFERENTIATING AMONG DOCUMENTS

Rome (Esau, Edom) in the Mishnah and Tractate Abot

If we ask the Mishnah, ca. 200 C.E. its principal view of the world beyond, it answers with a simple principle: the framers of the document insist that the world beyond was essentially undifferentiated. Rome to them proved no more and no less important than any other place in that single world. So far as the epochs of human history were concerned, these emerged solely from within Israel, and in particular the history of Israel's cult, as *m. Zeb.* 14:4–9 lays matters out in terms of the cult's location, and *m. Rosh. Hash.* 4:1–4 in terms of the before and after of the destruction.[4] The undifferentiation of the outside world is due to the simple fact that the entire earth outside of the Land of Israel in the Mishnah's law was held to suffer from contamination by corpses. Hence it was unclean with a severe mode of uncleanness, inaccessible to the holy and life-sustaining processes of the cult. If an Israelite artist were asked to paint a wall portrait of the world beyond the Land, he would paint the entire wall white, the color of death. Among corpses, how are we to make distinctions? We turn then to how the Mishnah and tractate Abot treat Rome both directly and in the symbolic form of Esau and Edom. Since the system at hand treats all gentiles as essentially the same, Rome, for its part, will not present a theme of special interest. So if my description of the Mishnah's basic mode of differentiation among outsiders proves sound, then Rome should not differ vastly from other outsiders.

As a matter of fact, if we turn to H. Y. Kosovsky, *Thesaurus Mishnae* (Jerusalem, 1956) I, II, IV, and look for Edom, Esau, Ishmael, and

---

4. In my *Messiah in Context: Israel's History and Destiny in Formative Judaism*, Foundations of Judaism, vol. 2 (Philadelphia: Fortress Press, 1983), I dealt at some length with the larger question of the later reimagining of Israel's history. But that is not at issue here.

Rome, we come away disappointed. "Edom" in the sense of Rome does not occur. The word stands for the Edomites of biblical times (*m. Yebam.* 8:3) and the territory of Edom (*m. Ketub.* 5:8). Ishmael, who like Edom later stands for Rome, supplies a name of a sage, nothing more. As to the term Rome itself, the picture is not terribly different. There is a "Roman hyssop," (*m. Parah.* 11:7, *m. Neg.* 14:6), and Rome occurs as a place-name (*m. Abod. Zarah.* 4:7). Otherwise I see not a single passage indicated by Kosovsky in which Rome serves as a topic of interest, and, it goes without saying, in no place does "Rome" stand for an age in human history, let alone the counterpart to and opposite of Israel. Rome is part of the undifferentiated other, the outside world of death. That fact takes on considerable meaning when we turn to the later fourth and fifth century compilations of scriptural exegeses. But first, we turn to the Mishnah's closest companion, the Tosefta.

Rome in the Tosefta

When we come to the Tosefta, a document containing systematic and extensive supplements to the sayings of the Mishnah, we find ourselves entirely within the Mishnah's circle of meanings and values. When, therefore, we ask how the Tosefta's authors incorporate and treat apocalyptic verses of Scripture, as they do, we find that they reduce to astonishingly trivial and local dimensions materials bearing for others world-historical meaning—including symbols later invoked by the sages themselves to express the movement and meaning of history. No nation, including Rome, plays a role in the Tosefta's interpretation of biblical passages presenting historical apocalypse, as we now see in the Tosefta's treatment of the apocalyptic vision of Daniel. There we find that history happens in what takes place in the sages' debates—there alone! We turn to the usage of the words Esau, Edom, Ishmael, and Rome, which in just a moment will come to center stage. Relying on H. Y. Kosovsky [here: Chaim Josua Kasowski], *Thesaurus Thosephthae* (Jerusalem, I: 1932; III: 1942; VI: 1961), we find the same sort of usages, in the same proportions, as the Mishnah has already shown us. Specifically, Edom is a biblical people, *t. Yebam.* 8:1, *Nid.* 6:1, *Qidd.* 5:4. Ishmael is a proper name for several sages. More important, Ishmael never stands for Rome. And Rome itself?

We have an individual, Todor of Rome (*t. Besa.* 2:15), Rome as a place where people live, for example, "I saw it in Rome" (*t. Yoma* 3:8), "I taught this law in Rome" (*t. Nid.* 7:1; *t. Miqw.* 4:7), and that is all.

If we were to propose a thesis on "Rome" and "Christianity" in the Talmud and midrash based on the evidence at hand, it would not produce many propositions. Rome is a place, and no biblical figures or places prefigure the place of Rome in the history of Israel. That is so even though the authors of the Mishnah and the Tosefta knew full well who had destroyed the Temple and closed off Jerusalem and what these events had meant. Christianity plays no role of consequence; no one takes the matter very seriously. Christians are people who know the truth but deny it: crazies. To state the negative: Rome does not stand for Israel's nemesis and counterpart, Rome did not mark an epoch in the history of the world, Israel did not encompass Rome in Israel's history of humanity, and Rome did not represent one of the four monarchies—the last, the worst—prior to Israel's rule. To invoke a modern category, Rome stood for a perfectly secular matter: a place, where things happened. Rome in no way symbolized anything beyond itself. And Israel's sages did not find they had to take seriously the presence or claims of Christianity.[5]

Rome in Genesis Rabbah

So much for books brought to closure, in the case of the Mishnah, at ca. 200 C.E., and, in the case of the Tosefta a hundred years later (no one knows). We come now to the year 400 or so, to the documents produced in the century after such momentous events as first, the conversion of Constantine to Christianity, and second, the catastrophe of Julian's failure in allowing the Temple to be rebuilt, the repression of paganism, and its effect on Judaism, the Christianization of the holy land, and, it appears, the conversion of sizeable numbers of Jews in the Land of Israel to Christianity and the consequent Christianization of Palestine (no longer, in context, the Land of Israel at all). We turn first to Genesis Rabbah, generally assigned to the year 400.

5. The dogma that Christianity never made a difference to Judaism confused me, too, as I shall point out presently.

In Genesis Rabbah the sages read the Book of Genesis as if it portrayed the history of Israel and Rome—and Rome in particular. Now Rome plays a role in the biblical narrative, with special reference to the counterpart and opposite of the patriarchs, first Ishmael, then Esau, and, always, Edom. For that is the single obsession binding the sages of the document at hand to common discourse with the text before them. Why Rome in the form it takes in Genesis Rabbah? And why the obsessive character of the sages' disposition of the theme of Rome? If their picture were merely of Rome as tyrant and destroyer of the Temple, we should have no reason to link the text to the problems of the age of redaction and closure. But now it is Rome as Israel's brother, counterpart, and nemesis, Rome as the one thing standing in the way of Israel's, and the world's, ultimate salvation. So the stakes are different, and much higher.

Let us take a simple example of how ubiquitous is the shadow of Ishmael/Esau/Edom/Rome. Wherever the sages reflect on future history, their minds turn to their own day. They found the hour difficult because Rome, now Christian, claimed that very birthright and blessing which they understood to be theirs alone. Christian Rome posed a threat without precedent. Now another dominion beside Israel's claimed the rights and blessings that sustained Israel. Wherever they turned in Scripture, the sages found comfort in the iteration that the birthright, the blessing, the Torah, and the hope, all belonged to them and to none other. Here is a striking statement of that constant proposition.

LIII:XII

   2.A. "But God said to Abraham, 'Be not displeased because of the lad and because of your slave woman; whatever Sarah says to you, do as she tells you, for through Isaac shall your descendants be named'" (Gen. 21:12):
   B. Said R. Yudan bar Shillum, "What is written is not 'Isaac' but 'through Isaac' [The matter is limited, not through all of Isaac's descendants but only through some of them, thus excluding Esau]."

The interpreter takes up the limiting particle, "in," that is, *among* the descendants of Isaac will be found Abraham's heirs, but not all the descendants of Isaac will be heirs of Abraham. Number 2 explicitly excludes Esau, that is, Rome. In the next passage Rome appears as a pig, an important choice for symbolization, as we shall see in Leviticus Rabbah as well:

LXV:I

1. A. "When Esau was forty years old, he took to wife Judith, the daughter of Beeri, the Hittite, and Basemath the daughter of Elon the Hittite; and they made life bitter for Isaac and Rebecca" (Gen. 26:34–35):

   B. "The swine out of the wood ravages it, that which moves in the field feeds on it" (Ps. 80:14).

   C. R. Phineas and R. Hilqiah in the name of R. Simon: "Among all of the prophets, only two of them spelled out in public [the true character of Rome, represented by the swine], Asaf and Moses.

   D. "Asaf: 'The swine out of the wood ravages it.'

   E. "Moses: 'And the swine, because he parts the hoof' (Deut. 14:8).

   F. "Why does Moses compare Rome to the swine? Just as the swine, when it crouches, puts forth its hooves as if to say, 'I am clean,' so the wicked kingdom steals and grabs, while pretending to be setting up courts of justice.

   G. "So Esau, for all forty years, hunted married women, ravished them, and when he reached the age of forty, he presented himself to his father, saying, 'Just as father got married at the age of forty, so I shall marry a wife at the age of forty.'

   H. " 'When Esau was forty years old, he took to wife Judith, the daughter of Beeri, the Hittite, and Basemath the daughter of Elon the Hittite.' "

How long would Rome rule? When would Israel succeed? The important point is that Rome was next to last, Israel last. Rome's triumph brought assurance that Israel would be next—and last:

LXXV:IV

2. A. "And Jacob sent messengers before him":

   B. To this one [Esau] whose time to take hold of sovereignty would come before him [namely, before Jacob, since Esau would rule, then Jacob would govern].

   C. R. Joshua b. Levi said, "Jacob took off the purple robe and threw it before Esau, as if to say to him, 'Two flocks of starlings are not going to sleep on a single branch' [so we cannot rule at the same time]."

3. A. ". . . to Esau his brother":

   B. Even though he was Esau, he was still his brother.

Esau remains Jacob's brother, and Esau rules before Jacob will rule.
The application to contemporary affairs cannot be missed, both in the
recognition of the true character of Esau—a brother!—and in the
interpretation of the future.

To conclude: Genesis Rabbah reached closure, people generally
agree, toward the end of the fourth century. That century marks the
beginning of the West as we have known it. Why so? Because in the
fourth century, from the conversion of Constantine and over the next
hundred years, the Roman Empire became Christian—and with it, the
West. So the fourth century marks the first century of the history of
the West in that form in which the West would flourish to our own
day. Accordingly, we should not find surprising the sages' recurrent
references, in the reading of Genesis, to the struggle of two equal powers, Rome and Israel, Esau and Jacob, Ishmael and Isaac. The world-
historical change, marking the confirmation in politics and power of
the Christians' claim that Christ was king over all humanity, demanded from the sages an appropriate, and to Israel, persuasive
response.

Rome in Leviticus Rabbah

What we see in Leviticus Rabbah is consistent with what we have
already observed in Genesis Rabbah: how the sages absorb events into
their system of classification. So it is the sages that make history
through the thoughts they think and the rules they lay down. In such
a context, we find no interest either in the outsiders and their powers,
or in the history of the empires of the world, or, all the more so, in
redemption and the messianic fulfillment of time. What is the alternative to the use of the sort of symbols just now examined? Let us
turn to the relevant passages of Leviticus Rabbah:

XIII:V

9. A. Moses foresaw what the evil kingdoms would do [to Israel].
   B. "The camel, rock badger, and hare" (Deut. 14:7). [Compare:
      "Nevertheless, among those that chew the cud or part the hoof,
      you shall not eat these: the camel, because it chews the cud but
      does not part the hoof, is unclean to you. The rock badger, because
      it chews the cud but does not part the hoof, is unclean to you. And
      the hare, because it chews the cud but does not part the hoof, is

unclean to you, and the pig, because it parts the hoof and is cloven-footed, but does not chew the cud, is unclean to you" (Lev. 11: 4–8).]

C. The camel (GML) refers to Babylonia, [in line with the following verse of Scripture: "O daughter of Babylonia, you who are to be devastated!] Happy will be he who requites (GML) you, with what you have done to us" (Ps. 147:8).

D. "The rock badger" (Deut. 14:7)—this refers to Media.

E. Rabbis and R. Judah b. R. Simon.

F. Rabbis say, "Just as the rock badger exhibits traits of uncleanness and traits of cleanness, so the kingdom of Media produced both a righteous man and a wicked one."

G. Said R. Judah b. R. Simon, "The last Darius was Esther's son. He was clean on his mother's side and unclean on his father's side."

H. "The hare" (Deut 14:7)—this refers to Greece. The mother of King Ptolemy was named "Hare" [in Greek: lagos].

I. "The pig" (Deut. 14:7)—this refers to Edom [Rome].

J. Moses made mention of the first three in a single verse and the final one in a verse by itself [(Deut. 14:7, 8)]. Why so?

K. R. Yohanan and R. Simeon b. Laqish.

L. R. Yohanan said, "It is because [the pig] is equivalent to the other three."

M. And R. Simeon b. Laqish said, "It is because it outweighs them."

N. R. Yohanan objected to R. Simeon b. Laqish, "'Prophesy, there-fore, son of man, clap your hands [and let the sword come down twice, yea thrice]' (Ezek. 21:14)."

O. And how does R. Simeon b. Laqish interpret the same passage? He notes that [the threefold sword] is doubled (Ezek. 21:14).

10.A. [Gen. R. 65:1] R. Phineas and R. Hilqiah in the name of R. Simon: "Among all the prophets, only two of them revealed [the true evil of Rome], Assaf and Moses.

B. "Asaf said, 'The pig out of the wood ravages it' (Ps. 80:14).

C. "Moses said, 'And the pig, [because it parts the hoof and is cloven-footed but does not chew the cud]' (Lev. 11:7).

D. "Why is [Rome] compared to a pig?

E. "It is to teach you the following: Just as, when a pig crouches and produces its hooves, it is as if to say, 'See how I am clean [since I have a cloven hoof],' so this evil kingdom takes pride, seizes by violence, and steals, and then gives the appearance of establishing a tribunal for justice."

13.A. Another interpretation [now treating "bring up the cud" (GR) as "bring along in its train" (GRR)]:

B. "The camel" (Lev. 11:4)—this refers to Babylonia.

    C. "Which brings along in its train"—for it brought along another kingdom after it.
    D. "The rock badger" (Lev. 11:5)—this refers to Media.
    E. "Which brings along in its train"—for it brought along another kingdom after it.
    F. "The hare" (Lev. 11:6)—this refers to Greece.
    G. "Which brings along in its train"—for it brought along another kingdom after it.
    H. "The pig" (Lev. 11:7)—this refers to Rome.
    I. "Which does not bring along in its train"—for it did not bring along another kingdom after it.
    J. And why is it then called "pig" (HZYR)? For it restores (MHZRT) the crown to the one who truly should have it [namely, Israel, whose dominion will begin when the rule of Rome ends].
    K. That is in line with the following verse of Scripture: "And saviors will come up on Mount Zion to judge the Mountain of Esau [Rome], and the kingdom will then belong to the Lord" (Obad. 21).

The first claim is that God had told the prophets what would happen to Israel at the hands of the pagan kingdoms, Babylonia, Media, Greece, Rome. These are further represented by Nebuchadnezzar, Haman, Alexander for Greece, Edom or Esau, interchangeably, for Rome. The same vision came from Adam, Abraham, Daniel and Moses. The same policy toward Israel—oppression, destruction, enslavement, alienation from the true God—emerged from all four. How does Rome stand out? First, it was made fruitful through the prayer of Isaac in behalf of Esau. Second, Edom is represented by the fourth and final beast. Rome is related through Esau, as Babylonia, Media, and Greece are not. The fourth beast was seen in a vision separate from the first three. It was worst of all and outweighed the rest. In the apocalypticizing of the animals of Lev. 11:4–8/Deut. 14:7 (the camel, rock badger, hare, and pig) the pig, standing for Rome, again emerges as different from the others and more threatening than the rest. Just as the pig pretends to be a clean beast by showing the cloven hoof, but in fact is an unclean one, so Rome pretends to be just but in fact governs by thuggery. Edom does not praise God but only blasphemes. It does not exalt the righteous but kills them. These symbols concede nothing to Christian monotheism and biblicism.

Of greatest importance, while all the other beasts bring further ones in their wake, the pig does not: "It does not bring another kingdom after it." It will restore the crown to the one who will truly deserve it, Israel. Esau will be judged by Zion, so Obadiah 21. Now how has the symbolization delivered an implicit message? It is in the treatment of Rome as distinct, but essentially equivalent to the former kingdoms. Beyond Rome, standing in a straight line with the others, lies the true shift in history, the rule of Israel and the cessation of the dominion of the (pagan) nations.

THE RESULT OF DIFFERENTIATION

When the sages of the Mishnah and the Tosefta spoke of Edom and Edomites, they meant biblical Edom, a people in the vicinity of the land of Israel. By Rome they meant the city—that alone. That fact bears meaning when we turn to documents produced two centuries later, and one hundred years beyond the triumph of Christianity. When the sages of Genesis Rabbah spoke of Rome, it was not a political Rome but a messianic Rome that is at issue: Rome as surrogate for Israel, Rome as obstacle to Israel. Why? It is because Rome now confronts Israel with a crisis, and, I argue, Genesis Rabbah constitutes a response to that crisis. Rome in the fourth century became Christian. The sages responded by facing that fact quite squarely and saying, "Indeed, it is as you say, a kind of Israel, an heir of Abraham as your texts explicitly claim. But we remain the sole legitimate Israel, the bearer of the birthright—we and not you. So you are our brother, Esau, Ishmael, Edom." And the rest follows.

By rereading the story of the beginnings, the sages discovered the answer and the secret of the end. Rome claimed to be Israel, and indeed, the sages conceded, Rome shared the patrimony of Israel. That claim took the form of the Christians' appropriation of the Torah as "the Old Testament," so the sages acknowledged a simple fact in acceding to the notion that, in some way, Rome too formed part of Israel. But it was the rejected part, the Ishmael, the Esau, not the Isaac, not the Jacob. The advent of the Christian Rome precipitated the sustained, polemical, and, I think, rigorous and well-argued rereading of beginnings in light of the end. Rome then marked the conclusion of human history as Israel had known it. Beyond? The coming of the true Messiah, the redemption of Israel, the salvation of the world, the end of time. So the issues were not inconsiderable, and when the sages spoke of Esau/Rome, as they did so often, they confronted the life or death decision of the day.

When we come to Leviticus Rabbah, we find ourselves several steps down the path explored by the compilers of Genesis Rabbah. The polemic represented in Leviticus Rabbah by the symbolization of Christian Rome, therefore, makes the simple point that first, Christians are no different from and no better than pagans; they are essentially the same. Second, just as Israel had survived Babylonia, Media, Greece, so would they endure to see the end of Rome (whether pagan, whether Christian). But of course the symbolic polemic rested on false assumptions, hence conveyed a message that misled Jews by misrepresenting their new enemy. The new Rome really did differ from the old. Christianity was not merely part of a succession of undifferentiated modes of paganism. True, the symbols assigned to Rome attributed worse, more dangerous traits than those assigned to the earlier empires. The pig pretends to be clean, just as the Christians give the signs of adherence to the God of Abraham, Isaac, and Jacob. That much the passage concedes. But it is not enough. For out of symbols should emerge a useful public policy, and the mode of thought represented by symbols in the end should yield an accurate confrontation with that for which the symbol stands.

This survey of four documents read one by one, then in pairs, yields a simple result. A striking shift in the treatment of Rome does appear to take place in the formative century represented by work on Genesis Rabbah and Leviticus Rabbah. In earlier times Rome symbolized little beyond itself, and Edom, Esau (absent in the Mishnah, a singleton in Tosefta), and Ishmael were concrete figures. In later times these figures bore traits congruent to the fact of Christian rule. The correspondence between the modes of symbolization—the pig, the sibling—and the facts of the Christian challenge to Judaism—the same Scripture, read a new way, the same messianic hope, interpreted differently—turns out to be remarkable and significant when we compare what the earlier compilers of canonical writings, behind the Mishnah and the Tosefta, produced to the writings of the later ones, behind the two Rabbah compilations. When we differentiate one document from the next, the details of each document turn out to cohere to the systemic traits of the document as a whole. And furthermore, what a document says about the common topic turns out to bear its own messages and meanings. That, in a single sentence, justifies the route of canonical differentiation which I advocated at the outset.

THE RESULT OF NOT DIFFERENTIATING: MISSING A DISTINCTION THAT MAKES A DIFFERENCE

When I originally worked on this problem, I took the view that the rabbinic canon, from beginning to end, fails to effect differentiation when it treats the outsider.[6] I maintained that the recognition of the outsider depends upon traits that, so far as the framers of the writings at hand are concerned, remain not only constant but uninteresting. The outsider is just that—not worthy of further sorting out. And, as a result of that premise, in the unfolding of canonical doctrine on the outsider, I did not discern substantial change from one document to the next. So, I concluded, people put out of mind that with which they cannot cope, and the outsider stood for the critical fact of Israelite life, the nation's weak condition and vanquished status. So for the same fundamental cause that accounts for the persistence among the founders of the Mishnah's system of the priestly conception of Israelite life, so too a single tight abstraction masked the detailed and concrete features of the other. All "others" looked alike—and posed a threat. The less response to that threat, the more comforting the illusion of inner control over an outer world wholly beyond one's power. In approaching matters as I did, I failed to see the traits stressed by the two Rabbah collections, traits specific to Rome as Christian and irrelevant to all other outsiders. I missed the message because I failed to compare what the Mishnah and the Tosefta say about Rome/Esau/Ishmael/Edom with what the two Rabbah compilations say about the

6. I refer to "Stable Symbols in a Shifting Society: The Delusion of the Monolithic Gentile in Documents of Late Fourth-Century Judaism," in *History of Religions*, 1985: 163–75. Cf. also Jacob Neusner and Ernest S. Frerichs, eds., *"To See Ourselves as Others See Us": Christians, Jews, "Others" in Late Antiquity* (Atlanta: Scholars Press, 1985), 373–96.

same matter. And the reason was that it never entered my mind that Christianity would make much difference to Judaism.

CONCLUSION

What went wrong? The answer is simple. I began my research with perfect faith in a dogma of Judaism and therefore also of scholars of Judaism. It is that Christianity never made any difference to Judaism. So I took for granted, without knowing it, that I too would find that Christianity never made any difference. My original results then conformed to the premise with which I had commenced. The error is not inconsequential. It is fundamental, because it is methodological. The methodological error is both general and specific. In general I erred by believing other people instead of asking how people knew the things they took for granted. I took over a prevailing attitude of mind—and I did not even realize it. The specific error was that I failed to work along lines I myself had already discovered. I homogenized what should be analyzed and differentiated. I gave "the talmudic view of . . ." having spent too many years trying to show that there is no such thing.

What is at stake? It is the progress of knowledge, learning as an active, continuing, progressive tense. I not only do not mind pointing out where I have erred, I take pleasure in doing so. That is why I do it all the time, and why I wonder at how rarely colleagues do so, that is, how little some people seem to learn both from others and from their own mistakes. They deprive themselves both of learning and of enjoyment. Why do I call it deprivation? Because there is pleasure in rethinking things, reworking conclusions and reconsidering questions earlier settled. It is one of the joys of learning as an ongoing and continuing, never-ending process.

Clearly, the documents read one by one do yield insight that combining all their statements on a given topic does not bring to light. So in sum, differentiating among documents shows us things that *not* differentiating among them obscures. Not seeing the books as individual statements obscured for me those shifts and turnings that now appear to respond to the movement of the wheel of history. And, it follows, that concerning both the outsider in general and Rome in particular, the history of Israel, properly analyzed, responded in a deep and systematic way to the single most considerable challenge the Jewish people in the Land of Israel was to face for the next fifteen hundred years: the rise of the Christian West as brother and enemy to Israel, the Jewish people.

6

Hermeneutical Change: Structures of Scriptural Exegesis

The exegesis of verses of Scripture defined a convention in Israelite life even before books of holy writings attained the status of Scripture. The relationship of Chronicles to Samuel and Kings shows us how within the life of ancient Israel people read one book in the light of some other, imposing an issue important to themselves upon writings of the remote past. Every known Judaism in ancient times, whether revealed in the writings of a sect (such as at Qumran among the Essenes), or in those of a philosopher (such as Philo), undertook to interpret verses of Scripture as part of the labor of defining the Judaism at hand, its worldview and way of life. No one can imagine that because the Mishnah rarely cites proof texts of Scripture for its propositions of law and analytical list-making the authors of the Mishnah, early and late, took no interest in reading passages of Scripture.

But from the framing of the Mishnah in the late second century until the fourth, a period of not under a century and probably as much as two centuries, the heirs and continuators of the Mishnah so far as we know did not make collections of verses of Scripture. That fact gains critical importance when we realize that it was through the work of compilation and redaction, not merely episodic exegesis, that formative minds of diverse kinds of Judaism made their points. Exegesis of verses of Scripture registered at the level of redaction, not merely through discrete remarks on this and that. Rather, it was by means of composing collections of such remarks into systematic and pointed statements that the treatment of individual verses took on the dignity of hermeneutics.

The framer of the passage constructed his unit of discourse wholly congruent with the purpose for which he undertook the exegesis of the discrete verses of the passage. If he wished to read the verses of Scripture in light of events, he organized his unit of discourse around the sequence of verses of Scripture under analysis. Had he wanted, he might have provided a sequential narrative of what happened, then inserted the verse he found pertinent, thus: "X happened, and that is the meaning of (biblical verse) Y." Such a mode of organizing exegeses served the school of Matthew. The purpose of exegesis makes a deep impact not only upon the substance of the exegesis but also and especially upon the mode of organizing the consequent collection of exegesis.

We find in the literary composition of the school of Matthew a powerful effort to provide an interpretation of verses of Scripture in line with a distinct program of interpretation. Furthermore, the selection and arrangement of these scriptural exegeses turn out to be governed by the large-scale purpose of the framers of the document as a whole. To illustrate these two facts four parallel passages are presented in which we find a narrative culminating in the citation of a verse of Scripture, hence a convention of formal presentation of ideas, style, and composition alike. In each case the purpose of the narrative is fulfilled not only in itself, but also in a subscription linking the narrative to the cited verse and stating explicitly that the antecedent narrative serves to fulfill the prediction contained in the cited verse, hence a convention of theological substance. We deal with Matthew 1:18–23, 2:1–6, 2:16–18, and 3:1–3.

Matt. 1:18–23

Now the birth of Jesus Christ took place in this way. When his mother Mary had been betrothed to Joseph, before they came together she was found to be with child of the Holy Spirit; and her husband Joseph, being a just man and unwilling to put her to shame, resolved to divorce her quietly. But as he considered this, behold, an angel of the Lord appeared to him in a dream, saying, "Joseph, son of David, do not fear to take Mary your wife, for that which is conceived in her is of the Holy Spirit;

she will bear a son, and you shall call his name Jesus, for he will save his people from their sins." All this took place to fulfill what the Lord had spoken by the prophet: "Behold, a virgin shall conceive and bear a son, and his name shall be called Emmanuel" (which means, God with us).

Matt. 2:1–6

Now when Jesus was born in Bethlehem of Judea in the days of Herod the king, behold, wise men from the East came to Jerusalem, saying, "Where is he who has been born king of the Jews? for we have seen his star in the East, and have come to worship him." When Herod the King heard this, he was troubled, and all Jerusalem with him; and assembling all the chief priests and scribes of the people, he inquired of them where the Christ was to be born. They told him, "In Bethlehem of Judea; for so it is written by the prophet: 'And you, O Bethlehem, in the land of Judah, are by no means least among the rulers of Judah; for from you shall come a ruler who will govern my people Israel.'"

Matt. 2:16–18

Then Herod, when he saw that he had been tricked by the wise men, was in a furious rage, and he sent and killed all the male children in Bethlehem and in all that region who were two years old or under, according to the time which he had ascertained from the wise men. Then was fulfilled what was spoken by the prophet Jeremiah: "A voice was heard in Ramah, wailing and loud lamentation, Rachel weeping for her children; she refused to be consoled, because they were no more."

Matt. 3:1–3

In those days came John the Baptist, preaching in the wilderness of Judea, "Repent, for the kingdom of heaven is at hand." For this is he who was spoken of by the prophet Isaiah when he said, "The voice of one crying in the wilderness: Prepare the way of the Lord, make his paths straight."

The four passages reveal a stunningly original mode of linking exegeses. The organizing principle derives from the sequence of events of a particular biography rather than the sequence of verses in a given book of Scripture or of sentences of the Mishnah. The biography of the person under discussion serves as the architectonic of the composition of exegeses into a single statement of meaning. This mode of linking exegeses—composing them into a large-scale collection such as we have at hand in the earliest rabbinic compilations—stands in contrast to the way taken at Qumran on the one side, and among the fifth and sixth centuries' compilers of rabbinic collections of exegeses on the other.

The passages of Matthew indicate a distinctive choice on how to compose a "unit of discourse." The choice is dictated by the character and purpose of the composition at hand. Since the life of a particular person—as distinct from events of a particular character—forms the focus of discourse, telling a story connected with that life and following this with a citation of the biblical verse illustrated in the foregoing story constitutes the organizing principle of the several units of discourse, all of them within a single taxon. The taxon is not only one-dimensional. It also is rather simple in both its literary traits and its organizing principle. We discern extremely tight narration of a tale, followed by a citation of a verse of Scripture, interpreted only through the device of the explicit joining language: this (1) is what that (2) means.

What we see so clearly in the work of the school of Matthew is a simple fact. The work of making up units of discourse and the labor of collecting these units of discourse together express a single principle, make a single statement, carry out the purposes of a single polemic. Let us give proper emphasis to this point.

Three things go together: (1) the principles of exegesis, (2) the purposes of exegesis, and (3) the program of collecting and arranging exegeses.

Once we realize the centrality of the work of composition of exegeses of verses of Scripture into a cogent statement we may grasp the question at hand. It is important to be crystal-clear about the problem. Why—in particular within the circles of Talmudic rabbis in the fourth, fifth, and sixth centuries—did people begin to compile exegeses of Scripture and make books of them? That is a very limited, narrowly historical problem. The problem is *not* why Jews in general began to undertake exegesis of the Hebrew Scriptures. Many other kinds of Jews had done so, as we all know, certainly throughout the preceding thousand years back to the sixth century c.e. Since the Hebrew Bible itself is rich in exegetical materials (for example, the books of Chronicles constitute a systematic commentary and revision of the books of Kings), we cannot ask why at just this time people read and interpreted Scriptures. Judaism had always done that.

Nor was there anything new even in collecting exegeses and framing them for a particular polemical purpose—creating a book out of comments on the Scripture and in the form of a commentary. The Essene library at Qumran presents us with compositions of biblical commentary and exegesis, on the one side. As already illustrated, the school of Matthew provides a picture of another sort of exercise in systematic composition based on the amplification and application of Israel's ancient Scriptures, on the other. We recognize, moreover, that both Israelite communities—the Essenes and the Christian Jews around Matthew—produced their collections not merely to preserve opinions but to make important statements in a stunning way. We also know, surely in the instance of Matthew, that the power of a brilliantly composed exegetical collection and arrangement can make its impact even after two thousand years. That is why to begin with people made and preserved such collections and arrangements—to say what they believed God had told them.

But within the formation of the holy literature (the canon) of rabbinic Judaism in particular, so far as we know, no one before the fourth and fifth centuries had produced a composition of biblical exegeses formed into collections—holy books. The rabbinic movement had flourished for hundreds of years without making this type of book. By the fifth century in this kind of Judaism there were at least two other ways in which to compose books, represented first by the Mishnah and secondly by the Talmud of the Land of Israel ("Palestinian Talmud," "Yerushalmi" or Jerusalem Talmud). More importantly, the exegesis of Scripture itself had within rabbinical circles long constituted a well-established mode of thought and expression. The Talmud for its part is full of exegeses, but it is not organized as a book of scriptural exegeses.

Making such collections defined the natural next step in the process precipitated by the Mishnah and the exegesis of the Mishnah. The Talmud, the great work of exegesis of the Mishnah, set the pattern and shaped the mold. The compilers of the exegetical collections then followed the Talmud's pattern and conformed to the mold of exegesis of the Mishnah by the Talmud. They composed discourses for Scripture within precisely the same taxonomical framework as the Talmud's discourses for the Mishnah. So the context of the composition of *midrash* collections and the Talmud alike was defined by the Mishnah.

How so? The advent of the Mishnah in ca. 200 demanded that people explain the status and authority of the new document. The reason the document proved decisive in the history of Judaism from its time to ours is that to begin with it enjoyed the sponsorship of the autonomous ruler of the Jewish nation in the Land of Israel, Judah the patriarch, with the result that the Mishnah served purposes other than learning and speculative thought. At its very beginnings the Mishnah was turned into an authoritative law code: the constitution, along with Scripture, of Israel and its Land. Accordingly, when completed the Mishnah emerged from the schoolhouse and made its move into the politics, courts, and bureaus of the Jewish government of the Land of Israel. Men who mastered the Mishnah thereby qualified themselves as judges and administrators in the government of Judah the patriarch as well as in the government of the Jewish community of Babylonia. Over the next three hundred years the Mishnah served as the foundation for the formation of the system of law and theology we now know as Judaism.

The vast collection constituted by the Mishnah therefore demanded explanation: What is this book? How does it relate to the (written) Torah revealed to Moses at Mount Sinai? Under whose auspices and by what authority does the law of the Mishnah govern the life of Israel? These questions bear both political and theological implications. But to begin with the answers emerge out of an enterprise of exegesis. The reception of the Mishnah followed several distinct lines, each of them symbolized by a particular sort of book. Each book in turn offered its theory of the origin, character, and authority of the Mishnah. For the next three centuries these theories would occupy the attention of the best minds of Israel, the authorities of the two Talmuds and the numerous other works of the age of the seed-time of Judaism.

One line from the Mishnah stretched through the Tosefta, a supplement to the Mishnah, and the two Talmuds, one formed in the Land of Israel, the other in Babylonia, both serving as exegesis and amplification of the Mishnah.

The second line stretched from the Mishnah to compilations of biblical exegesis of three different sorts. First, there were exegetical collections framed in relationship to the Mishnah, in particular Sifra, on Leviticus, Sifre on Numbers, and Sifre on Deuteronomy. Second, exegetical collections were organized in relationship to Scripture with special reference to Genesis and Leviticus. Third, exegetical collections focused on constructing abstract discourse out of diverse verses of Scripture on a single theme or problem, represented by Pesiqta de Rab Kahana.

This simple catalogue of the types, range, and volume of creative writing over the three hundred years from the closure of the Mishnah indicates an obvious fact. The Mishnah stands at the beginning of a new and stunningly original epoch in the formation of Judaism. Like the return to Zion and the advent of Jesus in Israel, the Mishnah ignited a great burst of energy. The extraordinary power of the Mishnah, moreover, is seen in its very lonely position in Israelite holy literature. The entire subsequent literature refers back to the Mishnah or stands in some clearcut hermeneutical relationship to it. But for its part the Mishnah refers to nothing prior to itself except (and then, mostly implicitly) to Scripture. So from the Mishnah back to the revelation of God to Moses at Sinai—in the view of the Mishnah—lies a vast desert. But from the Mishnah forward stretches a fertile plain.

Why should the Mishnah in particular have presented critical problems of a social and theological order? After all, it was hardly the first piece of new writing to confront Israel from the closure of Scripture to the end of the second century. Other books had found a capacious place in the canon of the groups of Israelites that received them and deemed them holy. The canon of some groups had made room for those writings of apocryphal and pseudepigraphic provenance so framed as to be deemed holy. The Essene library at Qumran encompassed a diverse group of writings, surely received as authoritative and holy, that other Jews did not know within their canon. So we have to stand back and ask why, to the sages who received and realized the Mishnah, that book should have presented special and particularly stimulating problems. Why should the issue of the relationship of the Mishnah to Scripture have proved so pressing in the third-, fourth-, and fifth-centuries' circles of Talmudic rabbis? After all, we have no evidence that the relationship to the canon of Scripture of the Manual of Discipline, the Hymns, the War Scroll, or the Damascus Covenant

perplexed the teacher of righteousness and the other holy priests of
the Essene community. To the contrary, those documents at Qumran
appear side by side with the ones we now know as canonical Scripture.
The high probability is that to the Essenes the sectarian books were
no less holy and authoritative than Leviticus, Deuteronomy, Nahum,
Habakkuk, Isaiah, and the other books of the biblical canon which
they revered, along with all Israelites.

The issue had to be raised because of the peculiar traits of the Mishnah itself. But the dilemma proved acute, not merely chronic, because
of the particular purpose the Mishnah was meant to serve and because
of the political sponsorship behind the document. It was to provide
Israel's constitution. It was promulgated by the patriarch—the ethnic
ruler—of the Jewish nation in the Land of Israel, Judah the Patriarch,
who ruled with Roman support as the fully recognized Jewish authority in the holy land. So the Mishnah was public, not sectarian,
nor merely idle speculation of a handful of Galilean rabbinical philosophers, though in structure and content that is precisely what it
was. It was a political document. It demanded assent and conformity
to its rules where they were relevant to the government and court
system of the Jewish people in its land. So the Mishnah could not be
ignored and therefore had to be explained in universally accessible
terms. Furthermore the Mishnah demanded explanation not merely
in relationship to the established canon of Scripture and apology as
the constitution of the Jew's government, the patriarchate of second-
century Land of Israel. The nature of Israelite life, lacking all capacity
to distinguish as secular any detail of the common culture, made it
natural to wonder about a deeper issue. Israel understood its collective
life and the fate of each individual under the aspect of God's loving
concern, as expressed in the Torah. Accordingly, laws issued to define
what people were supposed to do could not stand by themselves; they
had to receive the imprimatur of Heaven and be given the status of
revelation. And so to make its way in Israelite life the Mishnah as a
constitution and code demanded for itself a relationship to Sinai, with
Moses, from God.

However, the Mishnah stands in splendid isolation from Scripture
formally, redactionally, and linguistically. It is not possible to point
to many parallels in prior Israelite religious writing or cases of anony-

mous books, received as holy, in which the forms and formulations (specific verses) of Scripture play so slight a role. People who wrote holy books commonly imitated the Scripture's language. They cited concrete verses. They claimed at the very least that direct revelation had come to them, as in the angelic discourses of 4 Ezra and Baruch, so that what they say stands on an equal plane with Scripture. By contrast, the internal evidence of the Mishnah's sixty-two usable tractates (excluding Abot) in no way suggests that anyone pretended to talk like Moses and write like Moses or claimed to cite and correctly interpret things that Moses had said, or even alleged to have had a revelation like that of Moses and so to stand on the mountain with Moses. So the claim of scriptural authority for the Mishnah's doctrines and institutions is difficult to locate within the internal evidence of the Mishnah itself.

Let us now survey briefly the conceptual relationships between various Mishnah tractates on the one side, and laws of Scripture on the other.

First, there are tractates which simply repeat in their own words precisely what Scripture has to say and at best serve to complete the basic ideas of Scripture. For example, all of the cultic tractates of the Second Division, on Appointed Times (which tell what one is supposed to do in the Temple on the various special days of the year), and the bulk of the cultic tractates of the Fifth Division (which deal with Holy Things), simply restate facts of Scripture. For another example, all of those tractates of the Sixth Division on Purities which specify sources of uncleanness completely depend on information supplied by Scripture. Every important statement—for example, in Niddah (on menstrual uncleanness), in Zabim (on the uncleanness of the person with flux referred to in Leviticus 15), in Negaim (on the uncleanness of the person or house suffering the uncleanness described at Leviticus 13 and 14)—all of these tractates serve only to reiterate the basic facts of Scripture and to complement those facts with other derivative ones.

There are, second, tractates which take up facts of Scripture but work them out in a way that those scriptural facts could not have led us to predict. A supposition concerning what is important about the facts, utterly remote from the supposition of Scripture, will explain why the Mishnah tractates under discussion say the original things they say in confronting those scripturally provided facts. For example, Scripture (Num. 19:1–20) takes for granted that the red cow will be burned in a state of uncleanness because it is burned outside the camp (Temple). The Priestly writers cannot have imagined that a state of cultic cleanness was to be attained outside of the cult. The absolute datum of Mishnah tractate Parah (on burning the red cow), by contrast, is that cultic cleanness not only can be attained outside of the "tent of meeting"; the red cow was to be burned in a state of cleanness even exceeding the cultic cleanness required in the Temple itself. The problematic which generates the intellectual agendum of Parah, therefore, is how to work out the conduct of the rite of burning the cow in relationship to the Temple: Is it to be done in exactly the same way or in exactly the opposite way? This mode of contrastive and analogical thinking helps us to understand the generative problematic of such tractates of Erubin and Besah, to mention only two.

Third, there are many tractates that either take up problems in no way suggested by Scripture or begin from facts at best merely relevant to facts of Scripture. In the former category are Toharot, on the cleanness of foods, with its companion, Uqsin; Demai, on doubtfully tithed produce; Tamid, on the conduct of the daily whole-offering; Baba Batra, on rules of real estate transactions and certain other commercial and property relationships; and so on. Representative of the latter category is Oholot which spins out its strange problems within the theory that a tent and a utensil are to be compared to one another (!). Other instances are these: Kelim, on the susceptibility to uncleanness of various sorts of utensils; Miqwaot, on the sorts of water which effect purification from uncleanness; Ketubot and Gittin, on the documents of marriage and divorce; and many others. These tractates here and there draw facts of Scripture. But the problem confronted in these tractates—the generative problematic—in no way responds to issues or even facts important to Scripture. What we have here is a prior program of inquiry, which will make ample provision for facts of Scripture, generated essentially outside the framework of Scripture. First comes the problem or topic; then, if possible, attention to Scripture.

So some tractates merely repeat what we find in Scripture. Some are totally independent of Scripture. And some fall in between. We find everything and its opposite. But to offer a final answer to the question of Scripture-Mishnah relationships, we have to take that fact seriously. The Mishnah in no way is so remote from Scripture as its formal omission of citations of verses of Scripture suggests. It also cannot be described as contingent upon and secondary to Scripture, as many of its third-century apologists claimed. But the right answer is not that it is somewhere in between. Scripture confronts the framers of the Mishnah as revelation, not merely as a source of facts. But the framers of the Mishnah had their own world with which to deal. They made statements in the framework and fellowship of their own age and generation. They were bound, therefore, to come to Scripture with a set of questions generated elsewhere than in Scripture. They brought their own ideas about what was going to be important in Scripture. This is perfectly natural.

The philosophers of the Mishnah conceded to Scripture the highest authority. At the same time what they chose to hear within the authoritative statements of Scripture would in the end come from a statement of their own. All of Scripture was authoritative, but only some of Scripture was found to be relevant. And what happened is that the framers and philosophers of the tradition of the Mishnah came to Scripture when they had reason to. They brought to Scripture a program of questions and inquiries framed essentially among themselves. So they were highly selective. That is why their program itself constituted a statement *upon* the meaning of Scripture. They and their apologists of one sort hastened to add that their program consisted of a statement *of*, and not only upon, the meaning of Scripture.

The way in which the sages of the Mishnah utilized the inherited and authoritative tradition of Scripture therefore is clear. On the one hand, wherever they could they repeated what Scripture said. This they did, however, in their own words. So they established a claim of relevance and also authority. They spoke to their own day in their own idiom. On the other hand they selected with care and precision what they wanted in Scripture, ignoring what they did not want. They took up laws, not prophecies, descriptions of how things are supposed to be, not accounts of what is going to happen.

We turn now to ask how the heirs and continuators of the Mishnah, the rabbinical sages who inherited the document after ca. 200 C.E., sorted out the diverse questions before them: the questions of (1) canon, (2) scriptural authority, and (3) revelation. They had to make a judgment on the place and authority of the Mishnah within the total corpus of revelation ("the Torah"). In order to reach such an assessment they further had to impose their own view through exegesis of the Mishnah, about the place and authority of Scripture within the Mishnah, forming a concomitant position on the relationship of the Mishnah to Scripture. We now take up the principal documents produced in the rabbinical estate after the closure of the Mishnah.

As indicated earlier, different kinds of literature flow from the Mishnah and refer to it. The Tosefta supplements the Mishnah and relies upon the Mishnah for the whole frame of organization and redaction for all materials. The Sifra, exegeses of Leviticus, focuses not upon the Mishnah but upon Scripture and proposes to provide a bridge between the two. Sifra, and to a lesser degree, Sifre to Numbers and Sifre to Deuteronomy, fall into this second category. The last is in the middle, both dependent upon and autonomous of the Mishnah, taking up its individual statements and amplifying them, but also expanding and developing autonomous discussions. The two Talmuds, one produced in the Land of Israel, the other in Babylonia, constitute this kind of writing.

The Tosefta makes no systematic effort to adduce scriptural proof texts for Mishnaic statements. The Sifra commonly attempts to show the Mishnah's links to the Scripture so that whatever is right in the Mishnah derives from, is secondary to, statements of Scripture. The Talmud takes up a far more complex position in rough balance between these two extreme views.

The important point of hermeneutical consequence concerns redaction. Work on the formulation and redaction of exegeses of the Mishnah, under way from the end of the second century, provided the model for work on the composition of exegeses of Scripture. What the exegetes had been doing for upwards of two centuries for the Mishnah, their successors and heirs began to do only in the fourth and fifth centuries for Scripture: make up well-organized compositions of scriptural exegeses. What the exegetes did for the Mishnah they did later on for Scripture.

Taking Genesis Rabbah as the model, since that document comes in midcourse between Sifra and the two Sifres (one for Numbers, the other for Deuteronomy), which reached closure before the fourth century, and Leviticus Rabbah and its successors Lamentations Rabbati and Pesiqta de Rab Kahana and the like, which came to conclusion from the mid-fifth century onward, what do we see? It is that Genesis Rabbah, the document universally regarded as the first compilation of exegeses accomplished within the rabbinical circles in particular, is composed of units of discourse as cogent in their way as the ones in the Talmud of the Land of Israel. These units of discourse fall into precisely the same taxonomical categories as those of the Talmud of the Land of Israel. Accordingly, the way in which the rabbinical exegetes who selected passages of the Mishnah and so constructed the Talmud of the Land of Israel did their exegetical work turns out to be the same as the way in which rabbinical exegetes who selected passages of Scripture and so constructed Genesis Rabbah did their work. Self-evidently, what the one group had to say about the Mishnah bears no material relationship to what the other group had to say about Genesis. But the modes of thought, the ways of framing inquiries and constructing the results into formations of protracted and cogent discourse, serving quite specific and limited hermeneutical purposes—these are taxonomically uniform. Furthermore, the result is the same even when we employ a taxonomical system defined not by the Mishnah's continuum but solely by formal traits of Genesis Rabbah's units of discourse, specifically the placement of a verse of Scripture and the mode of analysis of that verse within an exegetical construction. What the masters of biblical exegesis did in Genesis was what the masters of Mishnah exegesis did for whatever Mishnah tractate they chose for study. It follows that the compiling of the first collection of biblical exegesis falls into the same intellectual framework as the Talmud of the Land of Israel, whether this was before, at the same time as, or in the aftermath of the composition of Yerushalmi.

The exegetes of Scripture and compilers of exegeses might have taken diverse tacks. The word *midrash* bears multiple and imprecise meanings. The activity of compiling such *midrash*, meaning exegesis of Scripture, turns out to express all of the differences among the diverse groups of ancient Israel which took up the work of framing their ideas in response to Scripture. Just as you could say anything you wanted about Scripture, so you could collect anything you wanted and call it *midrash* of any text you chose. *How* collections were made as much as *what* was compiled in them expressed the distinctive policy and program at hand.

In defining these taxonomical categories, we see there are four, of which the first two are closely related, and the fourth of slight consequence.

The first category encompasses close exegesis of Scripture by which is meant a word-for-word or phrase-by-phrase interpretation of a passage. In such an activity the framer of a discrete composition will wish to read and explain a verse or a few words of a verse of the Scripture at hand.

The second category, no less exegetical than the first, is made up of units of discourse in which the components of the verse are treated as part of a larger statement of meaning rather than as a set of individual phrases, stitches requiring attention one by one. Accordingly, in this taxon we deal with wide-ranging discourse about the meaning of a particular passage, hence an effort to amplify what is said in a verse. Here the amplification may take a number of different forms and directions. But the discipline imposed by the originally cited verse of Scripture will always impose boundaries on discourse.

The third taxon encompasses units of discourse in which the theme of a particular passage defines a very wide-ranging exercise. In this discussion the cited passage itself is unimportant. It is the theme that is definitive. Accordingly, in this third type we take up a unit of discourse in which the composer of the passage wishes to expand on a particular problem (merely) illustrated in the cited passage. The problem rather than the cited passage defines the limits and direction of discourse. The passage at hand falls away, having provided a pretext for the real point of concern.

The fourth and final taxon, also deriving from the Yerushalmi, takes in units of discourse shaped around a given topic but not intended to constitute cogent and tightly framed discourse on said topic. These units of discourse then constitute topical anthologies rather than carefully composed essays.

The further important fact of Genesis Rabbah is simply that it *is* made up of "units of discourse." That is to say, we do not have a

mere mass of discrete sayings in which the number of sentences is the
same as the number of completed thoughts. Rather, we can break up
chapters of Genesis Rabbah into a finite number of cogent discussions,
paragraphs, each with its beginning, middle, and end. Upon that simple and self-evident fact everything else rests. For what it means is that
the whole has been made up of parts. These parts in turn exhibit the
abilities not of mere collectors, but of masters of composition and
cogent reflection. So like the Talmud of the Land of Israel, Genesis
Rabbah's chapter at hand emerges in two stages: first, from people
who worked out its components; second, from people who arranged
them. These may well have been the same people, but the work was
in separate and distinct stages. First came the writing of compositions
expressive of complex ideas, framed in sophisticated ways. Second,
there was the work of selecting and arranging these units of discourse
into the composition now before us.

To summarize and conclude, the original work of collecting and
arranging the compilations of exegeses of Scripture followed the patterns set in collecting and arranging exegeses of the Mishnah. Just as
the Talmud (which is Mishnah exegesis) treats the Mishnah, so the
earliest collections of scriptural exegesis treat Scripture.

The character of the Mishnah itself and the context of its reception
defined the crisis and made it acute. The book was the first in Judaism
to ignore the character of antecedent holy literature, the marks of
consecration used by all former writers to gain for their writing the
status of holiness. Had the Mishnah remained an idle fantasy, a mere
philosophical vision of utopia, it would have presented no critical
theological problem. It also would never have come down to us—at
least not under the auspices of what became normative Judaism. But
the Mishnah rapidly found a chief place in the Jewish government of
the Land of Israel as the constitution and bylaws of the Jewish nation
in its land. Accordingly, the heirs of the Mishnah demanded for themselves a theory of its origin to validate its claim to authority and es-
tablish its grounds for compelling obedience whether in sanctions or
in a myth of supernatural origin in revelation.

The Mishnah therefore gradually made its way into the framework
of revealed law. It found for itself ample place within the category of
torah (revelation) and ultimately within the Torah itself (the canon of

Judaism). The route took the exegetes of the Mishnah squarely into the heart of the matter, the already available written Torah of Moses. Now as we have observed at some length, the path from the Mishnah to the Torah hardly runs straight and true. For the Mishnah frames its ideas in modes different from those of the written Torah's law codes. And many of its ideas and points of emphasis indeed proved alien to those of Scripture. Always in style and often in substance, the Mishnah appears to be anything but an appendage to the Mosaic law codes.

How to pave the road from the Mishnah to Scripture? The answer lay in one age-old and commonplace mode of dealing with precisely the same problem. A conventional way of reading Scripture commonly called *midrash* and here called simply *exegesis* had long proved acceptable. Why change now? As we know full well, Israelite thinkers routinely read one thing in relationship to something else, old Scripture in the setting of fresh concerns and sure knowledge of new truth. So there is nothing remarkable in what the heirs of the Mishnah did. To seek through biblical exegesis to link the Mishnah to Scripture, detail by detail, followed a well-trodden path.

Work on Scripture, merely routinely encompassing the scriptual basis for the Mishnah's statements, represents one extreme. The Mishnah by itself required no systematic linkage to Scripture. Or work on Scripture repeatedly demanded attention to laws in the Mishnah with the polemical implication that the latter without the former stood naked. This stands at the opposite extreme. Work on Scripture in the assumption that support for the Mishnah should derive from Scripture represented the third and mediating position. It is not a polemic but an assertion of veneration. So to the Tosefta, Sifra, and Talmud of the Land of Israel alike, the paramount issue was Scripture, not merely its authority, but especially its sheer mass of information. The decisive importance of the advent of the Mishnah in precipitating the exegetical enterprise represented by the books at hand emerges from a simple fact. The documents before us all focus attention on the Mishnah in Israel (not to mention the other larger Talmud made in Babylonia) and organize everything at hand around the redactional structure supplied by the Mishnah itself. The Sifra's obsession with the Mishnah is still more blatant.

For it is all the more striking what the redactional choice of the Sifra's framers called to the fore: the selection of a book of Scripture rather than a tractate of the Mishnah as the focus for exegesis and for organizing it. That choice conforms entirely to the polemic of the writers and compilers of the Sifra: Scripture is important, the Mishnah subordinate. How better to say so than to organize things not around the Mishnah but around a book of the law of Moses itself? So the Mishnah is now cited in a work about Scripture.

Down to the editing of the Sifra Scripture had been cited in works on the Mishnah. Since the Sifra draws upon materials of the Mishnah and the Tosefta, we have every reason to suppose the redactors of the Sifra knew full well the ways taken by others. They rejected those ways, reversing the redactional convention based on the Mishnah's structure and choosing what was, in context, a fresh and different route. In the setting of antecedent Judaism, that route had been entirely familiar. Earlier writers had laid out their exegesis of Scripture side by side with a text of Scripture. So doing things the way the Sifra's composers did the work was nothing new. Earlier writers also had expressed their own ideas through their arrangement of verses of Scripture.

But the Mishnah is the first document of its kind in Judaism. Afterward the Tosefta and the Talmud came along—probably at roughly the same time. Their materials derived both from the period in which the Mishnah was taking shape and also from the period after which the Mishnah had reached closure. And it would seem the Sifre comes later on, surely after both the Mishnah and the Tosefta. Its assertions are more extreme, its redactional definition more radical. We notice a correspondence, therefore, between the kind of material that is collected and the way that material is arranged. It follows that the polemical purposes of the document are expressed not only in what is said, but in how what is said is collected and arranged. That fact is more critical to the larger task of interpreting the context in which midrash collections come into being. For the late fourth- and fifth-century compositors joined the two available principles, the one of taxonomy of exegesis, the other of mode of composition, and began a wholly new venture.

They took up the choice of redactional principle introduced by the

Sifra's authorship (perhaps in tandem with the Sifres' authorships). They chose a biblical book rather than a Mishnah tractate for their focus of composition and organization. They took up the methods of hermeneutics fully worked out by the exegetes of the Mishnah in the Talmud of the Land of Israel. They followed the same taxonomic structure of exegesis. This they applied to the book of Genesis, later on to the book of Leviticus. So the structure of scriptural exegesis rests upon the foundations of Mishnah-exegesis worked out over the preceding century or two. What people said followed the patterns developed out of the work on the Mishnah. How they organized what they said followed the principles of composition developed from work on the relationship of the Mishnah to Scripture. But what they then did—systematic work on Genesis, then Leviticus—was wholly fresh, entirely their own.

7

Symbolic Change: The Transformation of the Torah

Judaism as we know it at the end of late antiquity reached its now familiar definition when "the Torah" lost its capital letter and definite article and ultimately became "*torah*." What for nearly a millennium had been a particular scroll or book thus came to serve as the symbol of an entire system. When a rabbi spoke of *torah* he no longer meant only a particular object; now he used the word to encompass a distinctive and well-defined worldview and way of life. Torah had come to stand for something one does. Knowledge of the Torah promised not merely information about what people were supposed to do but ultimate redemption or salvation.

The Torah of Moses clearly occupied a critical place in all systems of Judaism from the closure of the Torah-book, the Pentateuch, in the time of Ezra onward. But in late antiquity for one group alone the book developed into an abstract and encompassing symbol, so that in the Judaism that took shape in the formative age, the first seven centuries C.E., everything was contained in that one thing. How so? When we speak of *torah* in rabbinical literature of late antiquity we no longer denote a particular book on the one side, or the contents of such a book on the other. Instead we connote a broad range of clearly distinct categories of noun and verb, concrete fact and abstract relationship alike. "Torah" stands for a kind of human being. It connotes a social status and a sort of social group. It refers to a type of social relationship. It further denotes a legal status and differentiates among legal norms. As symbolic abstraction the word encompasses things and persons, actions and status, points of social differentiation and legal and normative standing, as well as "revealed truth." In all, the main points of insistence of the whole of Israel's life and history come to full symbolic expression in that single word. If people wanted to explain how they would be saved they would use the word Torah. If they wished to sort out their relationships with gentiles they would use the word Torah. Torah stood for salvation and accounted for Israel's this-worldly condition and the hope for both individual and nation alike of life in the world to come. For the kind of Judaism under discussion, therefore, the word Torah stood for everything. The Torah symbolized the whole. When we wish to describe the unfolding of the definitive doctrine of Judaism in its formative period, the first exercise consists in paying close attention to the meanings imputed to a single word.

Every detail of the religious system at hand exhibits essentially the same point of insistence captured in the notion of the Torah as the generative symbol, the total, exhaustive expression of the system as a whole. The definitive myth explained that one who studied Torah would become holy, like Moses "our rabbi," and like God in whose image humanity was made and whose Torah provided the plan and the model for what God wanted of a humanity created in his image. Whereas for Christians God was made flesh in Christ, the framers of the system of Judaism at hand found in the Torah that image of God to which Israel should aspire and to which the sage in fact conformed.

The several meanings of the Torah may be characterized succinctly.

When the Torah refers to a particular thing it is to a scroll containing divinely revealed words.

The Torah may refer further to revelation, not as an object but as a corpus of doctrine.

When one "does Torah" the disciple "studies" or "learns" and the master "teaches" Torah. Hence while the word Torah never appears as a verb, it does refer to an act.

The word also bears a quite separate sense, torah as category or classification or corpus of rules, for example, "the torah of driving a car" is a usage entirely acceptable to some documents. This generic usage of the word does occur.

The word Torah very commonly refers to a status (distinct from and above another status) in "teachings of Torah" as against "teachings of scribes." For the two Talmuds that distinction is absolutely critical to the entire hermeneutic enterprise. But it is important even in the Mishnah.

Obviously, no account of the meaning of the word Torah can ignore the distinction between the two Torahs, written and oral. It is important only in the secondary stages of the formation of the literature.

Finally, the word Torah refers to a source of salvation, often fully worked out in stories about how the individual and the nation will be saved through Torah. In general the sense of the word "salvation" is not complicated. It is simply salvation in the way in which Deuteronomy and the Deuteronomic historians understand it: kings who do what God wants win battles, those who do not, lose. So here too, people who study and do Torah are saved from sickness and death, and the way Israel can save itself from its condition of degradation also is through Torah.

Upon its closure the Mishnah gained an exalted political status as the constitution of Jewish government of the Land of Israel. Accordingly, the clerks who knew and applied its law had to explain the standing of that law, meaning its relationship to the law of the Torah. But the Mishnah provided no account of itself. Unlike biblical law codes the Mishnah begins with no myth of its own origin. It ends with no doxology. Discourse commences in the middle of things and ends abruptly. What follows from such laconic mumbling is that the exact status of the document required definition entirely outside the framework of the document itself. The framers of the Mishnah gave no hint of the nature of their book, so the Mishnah reached the political world of Israel without a trace of self-conscious explanation or any theory of validation.

The one thing that is clear, alas, is negative. The framers of the Mishnah nowhere claim, implicitly or explicitly, that what they have written forms part of the Torah, enjoys the status of God's revelation to Moses at Sinai, or even systematically carries forward secondary exposition and application of what Moses wrote down in the wilderness. Later on (two hundred years beyond the closure of the Mishnah) the need to explain the standing and origin of the Mishnah led some to posit two things. First, God's revelation of the Torah at Sinai encompassed the Mishnah as much as Scripture. Second, the Mishnah was handed on through oral formulation and oral transmission from Sinai to the framers of the document as we have it. These two convictions, fully exposed in the ninth-century letter of Sherira, in fact emerge from the references of both Talmuds to the dual Torah. One part is in writing. The other was oral and now is in the Mishnah.

As for the Mishnah itself, however, it contains not a hint that anyone has heard any such tale. The earliest apologists for the Mishnah, represented in Abot and the Tosefta, know nothing of the fully realized myth of the dual Torah of Sinai. It may be that the authors of those documents stood too close to the Mishnah to see the Mishnah's standing as a problem or to recognize the task of accounting for its origins. Certainly they never refer to the Mishnah as something out there, nor speak of the document as autonomous and complete. Only the two Talmuds reveal that conception—alongside their mythic explanation of where the document came from and why it should be obeyed. So the Yerushalmi marks the change. The absence of explicit expression of such a claim in behalf of the Mishnah requires little specification. It is just not there.

Nevertheless the absence of an implicit claim demands explanation. When ancient Jews wanted to gain the status of revelation (of *torah*) for their writings, or at least to link what they thought to what the Torah had said, they could do one of four things. They could sign the name of a holy man of old, for instance, Adam, Enoch, Ezra. They could imitate the Hebrew style of Scripture. They could claim that God had spoken to them. They could, at the very least, cite a verse of Scripture and impute to the cited passage their own opinion. These four methods—pseudepigraphy, stylistic imitation (hence forgery), claim of direct revelation from God, and eisegesis—found no favor with the Mishnah's framers. To the contrary, they signed no name to their book. Their Hebrew was new in its syntax and morphology, completely unlike that of the Mosaic writings of the Pentateuch. They never claimed that God had anything to do with their opinions. They rarely cited a verse of Scripture as authority. It follows that whatever the authors of the Mishnah said about their document the implicit character of the book tells us that they did not claim God had dictated or even approved what they had to say. Why not? The framers simply ignored all the validating conventions of the world in which they lived, and failed to make explicit use of any others.

It follows that we do not know whether the Mishnah was supposed to be part of the Torah or to enjoy a clearly defined relationship to the existing Torah. We also do not know what else, if not the Torah, was meant to endow the Mishnah's laws with heavenly sanction. To state matters simply, we do not know what the framers of the Mishnah said they had made, nor do we know what the people who received and were supposed to obey the Mishnah thought they possessed.

A survey of the uses of the word Torah in the Mishnah provides us with an account of what the framers of the Mishnah, founders of what would emerge as rabbinic Judaism, understood by that term. But it will not tell us how they related their own ideas to the Torah, nor shall we find a trace of evidence of that fully articulated way of life— the use of the word Torah to categorize and classify persons, places, things, relationships, all manner of abstractions—that we find fully exposed in some later redacted writings.

True, the Mishnah places a high value upon studying the Torah and upon the status of the sage. A *"mamzer*-disciple of a sage takes priority over a high-priest *am-haares,"* as at *m. Hor.* 3:8. But that judgment, distinctive though it is, cannot settle the question. All it shows is that the Mishnah pays due honor to the sage. But if the Mishnah does not claim to constitute part of the Torah, then what makes a sage a sage is not mastery of the Mishnah *in particular*. What we have merely continues the established and familiar position of the wisdom writers of old. Wisdom is important. Knowledge of the Torah is definitive. But to maintain that position one need hardly profess the fully artic- ulated Torah-myth of rabbinic Judaism. Proof of that fact, after all, is the character of the entire wisdom literature prior to the Mishnah itself.

So the issue is clearly drawn. It is not whether we find in the Mishnah exaggerated claims about the priority of the disciple of a sage. We do find such claims. The issue is whether we find in the Mishnah the assertion that whatever the sage has on the authority of his master goes back to Sinai. We seek a definitive view that what the sage says falls into the classification of Torah, just as what Scripture says constitutes Torah from God to Moses. That is what distinguishes wisdom from the Torah as it emerges in the context of rabbinic Judaism. To state the outcome in advance: we do not find the Torah in the Mishnah, and the Mishnah is not part of the Torah.

When the authors of the Mishnah surveyed the landscape of Israelite writings down to their own time, they saw only Sinai, that is, what we now know as Scripture. Based on the documents they cite or mention, we can say with certainty that they knew the pentateuchal law. We may take for granted that they accepted as divine revelation also the Prophets and the Writings, to which they occasionally make reference. That they regarded the Torah, Prophets, and Writings as a single composition, as revelation, appears from their references to *the Torah* as a specific "book," and to a Torah-scroll. Accordingly, one important meaning associated with the word Torah was concrete in the extreme. The Torah was a particular book or set of books, regarded as holy, revealed to Moses at Sinai. That fact presents no surprise, since the Torah-scroll(s) had existed, it is generally assumed, for many centuries before the closure of the Mishnah in 200.

What is surprising is that everything from the formation of the canon of the Torah to their own day seems to have proved null in their eyes. Between the Mishnah and Mount Sinai lay a vast, empty plain. From the perspective of the Torah-myth as they must have known it, from Moses and the prophets to before Judah the Patriarch, lay a great wasteland. So the concrete and physical meaning attaching to the word Torah as *the Torah*, the Torah revealed by God to Moses at Mount Sinai (including the books of the Prophets and the Writings), bore a contrary implication. Beyond *the Torah* there was no *torah*. Besides the Pentateuch, Prophets, and Writings, not only did no physical scroll deserve veneration, but no corpus of writings demanded obedience. So the very limited sense in which the words *the Torah* were used passed a stern judgment upon everything else, all the other writings that we know circulated widely, in which other Jews alleged that God had spoken and said "these things."

The range of the excluded possibilities that other Jews explored demands no survey. It includes everything, not only the Gospels (by

200 c.e. long since in the hands of outsiders), but secret books, history books, psalms, wisdom writings, rejected works of prophecy—everything excluded from any biblical canon by whoever determined there should be a canon. If the library of the Essenes at Qumran tells us what might have been, then we must regard as remarkably impoverished the (imaginary) library that would have served the authors of the Mishnah: the Book of Books, but nothing else. We seldom see so stern, so austere a vision of what commands the status of holy revelation among Judaisms over time. The tastes of the Mishnah's authors express a kind of literary iconoclasm, but with a difference. The literary icons did survive in the churches of Christendom. But in their own society and sacred setting, the judgment of Mishnah's authors would prevail from its time to ours. Nothing in the Judaisms of the heritage from the Hebrew Scripture's time to the Mishnah's day would survive the implacable rejection of the framers of the Mishnah, unless under Christian auspices or buried in caves. So when we take up that first and simplest meaning associated with the word Torah, "*the* Torah,*"* we confront a singular entity that exists with no other thing of similar kind.

We confront more than a closing off of ancient claims to the status of revelation. For at the other end, out of *the Torah* as a particular thing, a collection of books, would emerge a new and remarkably varied set of meanings. Possibilities first generated by the fundamental meaning imputed to the word Torah would demand realization. How so? Once the choice for the denotative meaning of *the Torah* became canonical in the narrowest possible sense, the ranges of connotative meaning imputed to the Torah stretched forth to an endless horizon. So the one concrete meaning made possible many abstract ones, all related to that single starting point. Only at the end shall we clearly grasp in a single tableau the entire vista of possibilities. To begin with, it suffices to note that the Mishnah's theory of the Torah not only closed but also opened many paths.

Abot draws into the orbit of Torah-talk the names of authorities of the Mishnah. But Abot does not claim that the Mishnah forms part of the Torah. Nor, obviously, does the tractate know the doctrine of the two Torahs. Only in the Talmuds do we begin to find clear and ample evidence of that doctrine. Abot, moreover, does not understand

by the word Torah much more than the framers of the Mishnah do.
Not only does the established classification scheme remain intact, but
the sense essentially replicates already familiar usages, producing no
innovation. On the contrary, there is a diminution in the range of
meanings.

Yet Abot in the aggregate *does* differ from the Mishnah. The difference has to do with the topic at hand. The other sixty-two tractates
of the Mishnah contain Torah-sayings here and there. But they do not
fall within the framework of Torah-discourse. They speak about other
matters entirely. The consideration of the status of Torah rarely pertains to that speech. Abot, by contrast, says a great deal about Torah-
study. The claim that Torah-study produces direct encounter with God
forms part of Abot's thesis about the Torah. That claim by itself will
hardly have surprised Israelite writers of wisdom books over a span
of many centuries—whether those assembled in the Essene commune
at Qumran on the one side, or those represented in the pages of Prov-
erbs and in many of the Psalms or even the Deuteronomistic circle on
the other.

A second glance at tractate Abot, however, produces a surprising
fact. In Abot Torah is instrumental. The figure of the sage, his ideals
and conduct, forms the goal, focus and center. Abot regards study of
Torah as what a sage does. The substance of Torah is what a sage
says. This state of affairs obtains whether or not the saying relates to
scriptural revelation. The content of the sayings attributed to the sages
endows those sayings with self-validating status. The sages usually do
not quote verses of Scripture and explain them, nor do they speak in
God's name. Yet it is clear that the sages talk Torah. If a sage says
something, what he says is Torah. More accurately, what he says falls
into the classification of Torah. Accordingly, Abot treats Torah-learning as symptomatic, an indicator of the status of the sage, hence as
merely instrumental.

The simplest proof of that proposition lies in the recurrent formal
structure of the document, the two things the framers of the document
never omit and always emphasize: (1) the *name* of the authority behind
a saying, from Simeon the Righteous on downward, and (2) the con-
nective-attributive *"says."* So what is important to the redactors is
what they never have to tell us. Because a recognized sage makes a

statement, what he says constitutes in and of itself a statement in the status of Torah.

To elaborate let us look at the opening sentences. "Moses received Torah," and it reached "the Men of the Great Assembly." "The three things" those men said bear no resemblance to anything we find in written Scripture. They focus upon the life of sagacity—prudence, discipleship, a fence around the Torah. And as we proceed we find time and again that while the word Torah stands for two things, divine revelation and the act of study of divine revelation, it produces a single effect, the transformation of unformed man into sage. One climax comes in Yohanan ben Zakkai's assertion that the purpose for which a man (an Israelite) was created was to study Torah, followed by his disciples' specifications of the most important things to be learned in the Torah. All of these pertain to the conduct of the wise man, the sage.

We have to locate the document's focus not on Torah but on the life of sagacity (including, to be sure, Torah-study). But what defines and delimits Torah? It is the sage himself. So we may simply state the tractate's definition of Torah: Torah is what a sage learns. Accordingly, the Mishnah contains Torah. It may well be thought to fall into the classification of Torah. But the reason is that authorities whose sayings are found in the Mishnah possess Torah from Sinai. What they say, we cannot overemphasize, is Torah. How do we know it? *It is a fact validated by the association of what they say with their own names.*

So we miss the real issue when we ask Abot to explain for us the status of the Mishnah or to provide a theory of a dual Torah. The framers of Abot do not address the status of the Mishnah. And the instrumental status of the Torah as well as of the Mishnah lies in the net effect of their composition: the claim that through study of the Torah sages enter God's presence. So study of Torah serves a further goal, that of forming sages. The theory of Abot pertains to the religious standing and consequence of the learning of the sages. To be sure, a secondary effect of that theory endows with the status of revealed truth things the sages say. But then it is because they say them, not because they have heard them in an endless chain back to Sinai. The fundament of truth is passed on through sagacity, not through already formulated and carefully memorized truths. That is why the single most important word in Abot also is the most common, the word *"says."*

At issue in Abot is not the Torah but the authority of the sage. It is that standing that transforms a saying into a Torah-saying, or to state matters more appropriately, that places a saying into the classification of the Torah. Abot then stands as the first document of the doctrine that the sage embodies the Torah and is a holy man, like Moses "our rabbi," in the likeness and image of God. The beginning is to claim that a saying falls into the category of Torah if a sage says it as Torah. The end will be to view the sage himself as Torah incarnate.

The Mishnah is held in the Talmud of the Land of Israel to be equivalent to Scripture (*Y. Hor.* 3:5). But the Mishnah is not called Torah. Still, once the Mishnah entered the status of Scripture, it would take but a short step to a theory of the Mishnah as part of the revelation at Sinai—hence oral Torah. In the first Talmud we find the first glimmerings of an effort to theorize in general, not merely in detail, about how specific teachings of Mishnah relate to specific teachings of Scripture. The citing of scriptural proof texts for Mishnah propositions, after all, would not have caused much surprise to the framers of the Mishnah; they themselves included such passages, though not often. But what conception of the Torah underlies such initiatives, and how do Yerushalmi sages propose to explain the phenomenon of the Mishnah as a whole? The following passage gives us one statement. It refers to the assertion at *m. Hag.* 1:8D that the laws on cultic cleanness presented in the Mishnah rest on deep and solid foundations in the Scripture.

Y. Hagigah 1:7

[V A] *The laws of the Sabbath [M. 1:8B]:* R. Jonah said R. Harma bar Uqba raised the question [in reference to M. Hag. 1:8D's view that there are many verses of Scripture on cleanness], "And lo, it is written only, 'Nevertheless a spring or a cistern holding water shall be clean; but whatever touches their carcass shall be unclean' (Lev. 11:36). And from this verse you derive many laws. [So how can M. 8:8D say what it does about many verses for laws of cultic cleanness?]"

[B]R. Zeira in the name of R. Yohanan: "If a law comes to hand and you do not know its nature, do not discard it for another one, for lo, many laws were stated to Moses at Sinai, and all of them have been embedded in the Mishnah."

The truly striking assertion appears at B. The Mishnah now is claimed to contain statements made by God to Moses. Just how these statements found their way into the Mishnah and which passages of the Mishnah contain them we do not know. That is hardly important, given the fundamental assertion at hand. The passage proceeds to a further and far more consequential proposition. It asserts that part of the Torah was written down and part was preserved in memory and transmitted orally. In context, moreover, that distinction must encompass the Mishnah, thus explaining its origin as part of the Torah. Here is a clear and unmistakable expression of the distinction between two forms in which a single Torah was revealed and handed on at Mount Sinai, part in writing, part orally.

While the passage below does not make use of the language *Torah*-in-writing and *Torah*-by-memory, it does refer to "the written" and "the oral." I believe myself fully justified in supplying the word Torah in square brackets. The reader will note, however, that the word Torah likewise does not occur at K, L. Only when the passage reaches its climax at M does it break down into a number of categories—Scripture, Mishnah, Talmud, laws, lore. There it makes the additional point that *everything* comes from Moses at Sinai. So the fully articulated theory of *two Torahs* (not merely one Torah in two forms) does not reach final expression in this passage. But short of explicit allusion to *Torah*-in-writing and *Torah*-by-memory, which we find mainly in the Talmud of Babylonia, the ultimate theory of Torah of formative Judaism is at hand in what follows.

Y. Hagigah 1:7

[V D] R. Zeirah in the name of R. Eleazar: "'Were I to write for him my laws by ten thousands, they would be regarded as a strange thing' (Hos. 8:12). Now is the greater part of the Torah written down? [Surely not. The oral part is much greater.] But more abundant are the matters which are derived by exegesis from the written [Torah] than those derived by exegesis from the oral [Torah]."

[E] And is that so?

[F] But more cherished are those matters which rest upon the written [Torah] than those which rest upon the oral [Torah].

. . . . . .

[J] R. Haggai in the name of R. Samuel bar Nahman, "Some teachings were handed on orally, and some things were handed on in writing, and we do not know which of them is more precious. But on the basis of that which is written, 'And the Lord said to Moses, Write these words; in accordance with these words I have made a covenant with you and with Israel' (Exod. 34:27), [we conclude] that the ones which are handed on orally are the more precious."

[K] R. Yohanan and R. Yudan b. R. Simeon—One said, "If you have kept what is preserved orally and also kept what is in writing, I shall make a covenant with you, and if not, I shall not make a covenant with you."

[L] The other said, "If you have kept what is preserved orally and you have kept what is preserved in writing, you shall receive a reward, and if not, you shall not receive a reward."

[M] [With reference to Deut. 9:10: "And on them was written according to all the words which the Lord spoke with you in the mount,"] said R. Joshua b. Levi, "He could have written, 'On them,' but wrote, 'And on them.' He could have written, 'All,' but wrote, 'According to all.' He could have written, 'Words,' but wrote 'the words.' [These then serve as three encompassing clauses, serving to include] Scripture, Mishnah, Talmud, laws, and lore. Even what an experienced student in the future is going to teach before his master already has been stated to Moses at Sinai."

[N] What is the Scriptural basis for this view?

[O] "There is no remembrance of former things, nor will there be any remembrance of later things yet to happen among those who come after" (Qoh. 1:11).

[P] If someone says, "See, this is a new thing," his fellow will answer him, saying to him, "this has been around before us for a long time."

Here we have absolutely explicit evidence that people believed part of the Torah had been preserved not in writing but orally. Linking that part of the Mishnah remains a matter of implication. But it surely comes fairly close to the surface, when we are told that the Mishnah contains Torah-traditions revealed at Sinai. From that view it requires only a small step to the allegation that the Mishnah is part of the Torah, the oral part.

To define the category of the Torah as a source of salvation as the Yerushalmi states matters, I point to a story that explicitly expresses the proposition that the Torah constitutes a source of salvation. In this story we shall see that because people observed the rules of the Torah they expected to be saved. And if they did not observe them they accepted their punishment. So the Torah now stands for something more than revelation and a life of study, and (it goes without saying) the sage now appears as a holy and not merely a learned man. This is because his knowledge of the Torah has transformed him. Accordingly, we deal with a category of stories and sayings about the Torah entirely different from what has gone before.

Y. Taanit 3:8

[II A] As to Levi ben Sisi: troops came to his town. He took a scroll of the Torah and went up to the roof and said, "Lord of the ages! If a single world of this scroll of the Torah has been nullified [in our town], let them come up against me, and if not, let them go their way."

[B] Forthwith people went looking for the troops but did not find them [because they had gone their way].

[C] A disciple of his did the same thing, and his hand withered, but the troops went their way.

[D] A disciple of his disciple did the same thing. His hand did not wither, but they also did not go their way.

[E] This illustrates the following apophthegm: You can't insult an idiot, and dead skin does not feel the scalpel.

What is interesting here is how taxa into which the word Torah previously fell have been absorbed and superseded in a new taxon. The Torah is an object: "He took a scroll. . . ." It also constitutes God's revelation to Israel: "If a single word. . . ." The outcome of the revelation is to form an ongoing way of life embodied in the sage himself: "A disciple of his did the same thing. . . ." The sage plays an intimate part in the supernatural event: "His hand withered. . . ." Now can we categorize this story as a statement that the Torah constitutes a particular object or a source of divine revelation or a way of life? Yes and no. The Torah here stands not only for the things we already have catalogued. It represents one more thing which takes in all the others. Torah is a source of salvation. How so? The Torah stands for or constitutes the way in which Israel saves itself from marauders. This straightforward sense of salvation would not have surprised the author of Deuteronomy.

In the canonical documents up to the Yerushalmi we look in vain for sayings or stories that fall into such a category. True, we may take for granted that everyone always believed that in general Israel would be saved by obedience to the Torah. That claim would not have surprised any Israelite writers from the first prophets down through the final redactors of the Pentateuch in the time of Ezra and onward through the next seven hundred years. But in the rabbinical corpus from the Mishnah forward, the specific and concrete assertion that by taking up the scroll of the Torah and standing on the roof of one's house, confronting God in heaven, a sage in particular could take action against the expected invasion—that kind of claim is not located, so far as I know, in any composition surveyed so far.

Yet we cannot claim that the belief that the Torah in the hands of the sage constituted a source of magical, supernatural, and hence salvific power simply did not flourish prior to ca. 400 C.E. We cannot show it, hence we do not know it. All we can say with assurance is that no stories containing such a viewpoint appear in any rabbinical document associated with the Mishnah. So what is critical here is not the generalized category—the genus—of the conviction that the Torah serves as the source of Israel's salvation. It is the concrete assertion— the speciation of the genus—that in the hands of the sage and under conditions specified the Torah may be utilized in pressing circumstances as Levi, his disciple, and the disciple of his disciple used it. That is what is new.

This stunningly new usage of Torah found in the Talmud of the Land of Israel emerges from a group of stories not readily classified in our established categories. All of these stories treat the word Torah (whether scroll, contents, or act of study) as source and guarantor of salvation. Accordingly, evoking the word Torah forms the centerpiece of a theory of Israel's history on the one side, and an account of the teleology of the entire system on the other. Torah indeed has ceased to constitute a specific thing or even a category or classification when stories about studying the Torah yield not a judgment as to status (i.e., praise for the learned man) but promise for supernatural blessing now and salvation in time to come.

To the rabbis the principal salvific deed was to "study Torah" by which they meant memorizing Torah-sayings by constant repetition and, as the Talmud itself amply testifies (for some sages), profound analytic inquiry into the meaning of those sayings. The innovation now is that this act of "study of Torah" imparts supernatural power of a material character. For example, by repeating words of Torah the sage could ward off the angel of death and accomplish other kinds of miracles as well. So Torah-formulas served as incantations. Mastery of Torah transformed the man engaged in Torah-learning into a supernatural figure who could do things ordinary folk could not do. The category of "Torah" had already vastly expanded to such a degree that through transformation of the Torah from a concrete thing to a symbol, a Torah-scroll could be compared to a man of Torah, namely, a rabbi. Now once the principle had been established that salvation would come from keeping God's will in general, as Israelite holy men had insisted for so many centuries, it was a small step for rabbis to identify their particular corpus of learning, namely, the Mishnah and associated sayings, with God's will expressed in Scripture.

The key to the first Talmud's theory of the Torah lies in its conception of the sage, to which that theory is subordinate. Once the sage reaches his full apotheosis as Torah incarnate then, but only then, the Torah becomes (also) a source of salvation in the present concrete formulation of the matter. That is why we traced the doctrine of the Torah in the salvific process by elaborate citation of stories about the sages, living Torahs exercising the supernatural power of the Torah, and serving like the Torah itself to reveal God's will. Since the sage embodied the Torah and gave the Torah, the Torah naturally came to stand for the principal source of Israel's salvation, not merely a scroll or a source of revelation.

The history of the symbolization of the Torah proceeds from its removal from the framework of material objects, even from the limitations of its own contents, to its transformation into something quite different and abstract, quite distinct from the document and its teachings. The Torah stands for this something more, particularly when it comes to be identified with a living person, the sage, and endowed with those particular traits which the sage claimed for himself. While we cannot say that the process of symbolization leading to the pure abstraction at hand moved in easy stages, we may still point to the stations that had to be passed in sequence. The word Torah reached the apologists for the Mishnah in its long-established meanings:

Torah-scroll, contents of the Torah-scroll. But even in the Mishnah itself these meanings provoked a secondary development: status of Torah as distinct from other (lower) status, hence Torah-teaching in contradistinction to scribal-teaching. With that small and simple step the Torah ceased to denote only a concrete and material thing—a scroll and its contents. It now connoted an abstract matter of status. And once made abstract the symbol entered a secondary history beyond all limits imposed by the concrete object, including its specific teachings, the Torah-scroll.

I believe that Abot stands at the beginning of this process. In the history of the word Torah as abstract symbol, a metaphor serving to sort out one abstract status from another regained concrete and material reality of a new order entirely. For the message of Abot was that the Torah served the sage. How so? The Torah indicated who was a sage and who was not. Accordingly, the apology of Abot for the Mishnah was that the Mishnah contained things the sages had said. What the sages said formed a chain of tradition extending back to Sinai. Hence it was equivalent to the Torah. The upshot is that words of the sages enjoyed the status of the Torah. What sages said was Torah *as much as what Scripture said was Torah*.

There were two forms in which the Torah reached Israel: one [Torah] in writing, the other [Torah] handed on orally, in memory. The final step, fully revealed in the Talmud, however, brought the conception of Torah to its logical conclusion: what the sage said was in the status of the Torah, was Torah, because the sage was Torah incarnate. So the abstract symbol now became concrete and material once more. We recognize the many diverse ways in which the Talmud stated that conviction. Every passage in which knowledge of the Torah yields power over this world and the next, capacity to coerce to the sage's will the natural and supernatural worlds alike, rests upon the same viewpoint.

The first Talmud's theory of the Torah carries us through several stages in the processes of the symbolization of the word Torah. First transformed from something material and concrete into something abstract and beyond all metaphor, the word Torah finally emerged once more in a concrete aspect as the encompassing and universal mode of stating the whole doctrine, all at once, of Judaism in its formative age.

While both the national and the individual dimensions of salvation mark the measure of the word Torah in the Babylonian Talmud, the national one proves the more interesting. For the notion of private salvation through Torah study and practice, of which we hear much, presents no surprise. When by contrast we find God saying, "If a man occupies himself with the study of Torah, works of charity, and prays with the community, I account it to him as if he had redeemed me and my children from among the nations of the world" (*b. Ber.* 8a), we confront a concept beyond the imagination of the framers of Abot and the other compositions of that circle. Still more indicative of the importance for Israel as a whole which was imputed to Torah-learning is the view that those who master the Torah do not require protection by this-worldly means. Rabbis need not contribute to the upkeep of the walls of a town, "because rabbis do not require protection" (*b. B.B.* 8a). Sayings such as these focus upon the individual who has mastered the Torah. But the supernatural power associated with the Torah here is thought to protect not the individual alone, but Israelites in general associated with the individual Torah-master. So, given the social perspective of the sages, all Israel enjoys salvation through the Torah.

8

Teleological Change: The Reconsideration of the Messiah

Within the Judaism born in the centuries after 70, the distinct traditions of priest, sage, and messianist were joined in a new way. In the person of the rabbi, holy man, Torah incarnate, avatar and model of the son of David, rabbinic Judaism found its sole overarching system. So the diverse varieties of Judaic piety present in Israel before 70 came to be bonded over the next several centuries in a wholly unprecedented way, with each party to the union imposing its logic upon the other constituents of the whole. The ancient categories remained. But they were so profoundly revised and transformed that nothing was preserved intact. Judaism as we know it, the Judaism of Scripture and Mishnah, Midrash and Talmud, thereby effected the ultimate transvaluation of all the values, of all the kinds of Judaism that had come before. Through the person and figure of the rabbi, the whole burden of Israel's heritage was renewed and handed on from late antiquity to the present day.

The character of the Israelite Scriptures, with their emphasis upon historical narrative as a mode of theological explanation, leads us to expect all Judaisms to evolve as deeply messianic religions. With all prescribed actions pointed toward the coming of the Messiah at the end of time, and all interest focused upon answering the historical-salvific questions ("how long?"), Judaism from late antiquity to the present day presents no surprises. Its liturgy evokes historical events

125

to prefigure salvation; prayers of petition repeatedly turn to the speedy coming of the Messiah; and the experience of worship invariably leaves the devotee expectant and hopeful. Just as rabbinic Judaism is a deeply messianic religion, secular extensions of Judaism have commonly proposed secularized versions of the focus upon history and have shown interest in the purpose and denouement of events. Teleology again appears as eschatology embodied in messianic symbols.

Yet for a brief moment a vast and influential document presented a kind of Judaism in which history did not define the main framework by which the issue of teleology took a form other than the familiar eschatological one, and in which historical events were absorbed through their trivialization in taxonomic structures into an ahistorical system. In the kind of Judaism in this document messiahs played a part. But these "anointed men" had no historical role. They undertook a task quite different from that assigned to Jesus by the framers of the Gospels. They were merely a species of priest, falling into one classification rather than another.

That document is the Mishnah, ca. 200 C.E., a strange corpus of normative statements which we may, though with some difficulty, classify as a law code or a school book for philosophical jurists. By ca. 600 C.E. a system of Judaism emerged in which the Mishnah as foundation document would be asked to support a structure at best continuous with but in no way fully defined by the outlines of the Mishnah itself.

Coming at the system from the asymmetrical endpoint, we ask the Mishnah to answer the questions at hand. What of the Messiah? When will he come? To whom in Israel will he come? And what must or can we do while we wait to hasten his coming? If we now reframe these questions and divest them of their mythic cloak, we ask about the Mishnah's theory of the history and destiny of Israel and the purpose of the Mishnah's own system in relationship to Israel's present and end: the implicit teleology of the philosophical law at hand.

Answering these questions out of the resources of the Mishnah is not possible. The Mishnah presents no large view of history. It contains no reflection whatever on the nature and meaning of the destruction of the Temple in 70 C.E., an event that surfaces only in connection with some changes in the law explained as resulting from the end of the cult. The Mishnah pays no attention to the matter of the end time.

The word "salvation" is rare, "sanctification" commonplace. More strikingly, the framers of the Mishnah are virtually silent on the teleology of the system; they never tell us why we should do what the Mishnah tells us, let alone explain what will happen if we do. Incidents in the Mishnah are preserved either as narrative settings for the statement of the law or, occasionally, as precedents. Historical events are classified and turned into entries on lists. True, events do make an impact. But it always is for the Mishnah's own purpose and within its own taxonomic system and rule-seeking mode of thought. To be sure, the framers of the Mishnah may also have had a theory of the Messiah and of the meaning of Israel's history and destiny. But they kept it hidden, and their document manages to provide an immense account of Israel's life without explicitly telling us about such matters.

The Messiah in the Mishnah does not stand at the forefront of the framers' consciousness. The issues encapsulated in the myth and person of the Messiah are scarcely addressed. The framers of the Mishnah do not resort to speculation about the Messiah as a historical-supernatural figure. So far as that kind of speculation provides the vehicle for reflection on salvific issues, or in mythic terms, narratives on the meaning of history and the destiny of Israel, we cannot say that the Mishnah's philosophers take up those encompassing categories of being: Where are we heading? What can we do about it? That does not mean questions found urgent in the aftermath of the destruction of the Temple and the disaster of Bar Kokba failed to attract the attention of the Mishnah's sages. But they treated history in a different way, offering their own answers to its questions.

By "history" I mean not merely events, but how events serve to teach lessons, reveal patterns, tell us what we must do and what will happen to us tomorrow. In that context some events contain richer lessons than others; the destruction of the Temple of Jerusalem teaches more than a crop failure, being kidnapped into slavery more than stubbing one's toe. Furthermore, lessons taught by events—"history" in the didactic sense—follow a progression from trivial and private to consequential and public. The framers of the Mishnah explicitly refer to very few events, treating those they do mention with a focus quite separate from the unfolding events themselves. They rarely create narratives; historical events do not supply organizing categories or

taxonomic classifications. We find no tractate devoted to the destruction of the Temple, no complete chapter detailing the events of Bar
Kokba nor even a sustained celebration of the events of the sages' own
historical lives. When things that have happened are mentioned, it is
neither to narrate nor to interpret and draw lessons from the events.
It is either to illustrate a point of law or to pose a problem of the
law—always *en passant,* never in a pointed way.

The Mishnah absorbs into its encompassing system all events, small
and large. The sages accomplish a vast labor of taxonomy, an immense
construction of the order and rules governing the classification of
everything on earth and in heaven. The disruptive character of history—one-time events of ineluctable significance—scarcely impresses
the philosophers. They find no difficulty in showing that what appears
unique and beyond classification has in fact happened before and so
falls within the range of trustworthy rules and known procedures.
Once history's components lose their distinctiveness then history as a
didactic intellectual construct, as a source of lessons and rules, also
loses all pertinence.

So lessons and rules come from sorting things out and classifying
them from the procedures and modes of thought of the philosopher
seeking regularity. To this labor of taxonomy the historian's way of
selecting data and arranging them into patterns of meaning to teach
lessons proves inconsequential. One-time events are not important.
The world is composed of nature and supernature. The laws that count
are those to be discovered in heaven and in heaven's creation and
counterpart, on earth. Keep those laws and things will work out. Break
them and the result is predictable: calamity of whatever sort will su-
pervene in accordance with the rules. But just because it is predictable
a catastrophic happening testifies to what has always been and must
always be, in accordance with reliable rules and within categories
already discovered and well explained. That is why the lawyer-phi-
losophers of the second century produced the Mishnah—to explain
how things are. Within the framework of well-classified rules, there
could be messiahs, but no single Messiah.

If the end of time and the coming of the Messiah do not serve to
explain for the Mishnah's system why people should do what the
Mishnah says, then what alternative teleology does the Mishnah's first

apologetic, Abot, provide? Only when we appreciate the clear answers given in that document, brought to closure at ca. 250, shall we grasp how remarkable is the shift which took place in later documents of the rabbinic canon to a messianic framing of the issues of the Torah's ultimate purpose and value. Let us see how the framers of Abot, in the aftermath of the creation of the Mishnah, explain the purpose and goal of the Mishnah: an ahistorical, nonmessianic teleology.

The first document generated by the Mishnah's heirs took up the work of completing the Mishnah's system by answering questions of purpose and meaning. Whatever teleology the Mishnah *as such* would ever acquire would derive from Abot, a collection of sayings by authorities who flourished in the generation after Judah the Patriarch (in all likelihood the document is of the mid-third-century rabbinic estate of the Land of Israel). Abot presents statements to express the ethos and ethic of the Mishnah and so provides a kind of theory.

Abot agreed with the other sixty-two tractates: history proved no more important here than it had been before. With scarcely a word about history and no account of events at all, Abot manages to provide an ample account of how the Torah—written and oral, thus in later eyes, Scripture and Mishnah—came down to its own day. Accordingly, the passage of time as such plays no role in the explanation of the origins of the document, nor is the Mishnah presented as eschatological. Occurrences of great weight ("history") are never invoked. How then does the tractate tell the story of Torah, narrate the history of God's revelation to Israel, encompassing both Scripture and Mishnah? The answer is that Abot's framers manage to do their work of explanation without telling a story or invoking history at all. They pursue a different way of answering the same question by exploiting a non-historical mode of thought and method of legitimation. *Teleology serves the purpose of legitimation,* and hence is accomplished in ways other than explaining how things originated or assuming that historical fact explains anything.

Disorderly historical events entered the system of the Mishnah and found their place within the larger framework of the Mishnah's orderly world. But to claim that the Mishnah's framers merely ignored what was happening would be incorrect. They worked out their own way of dealing with historical events, the disruptive power of which they not only conceded but freely recognized. Further, the Mishnah's authors did not intend to compose a history book, a work of prophecy, or an apocalypse. Even if they had wanted to narrate the course of events they could hardly have done so through the medium of the Mishnah. Yet the Mishnah presents its philosophy in full awareness of the issues of historical calamity confronting the Jewish nation. So far as the philosophy of the document confronts the totality of Israel's existence, the Mishnah by definition *also* presents a philosophy of history.

The Mishnah's subordination of historical events contradicts the emphasis of a thousand years of Israelite thought. The biblical histories, the ancient prophets, the apocalyptic visionaries all had testified that events themselves were important. Events carried the message of the living God. Events constituted history and explained Israel's destiny. An essentially ahistorical system of timeless sanctification, worked out through construction of an eternal rhythm that centered on the movement of the moon and stars and seasons, represented a life chosen by few outside the priesthood. Furthermore, the pretense that what *happens* matters less than what *is* testified against palpable and memorable reality. Israel had suffered enormous loss of life. The Talmud of the Land of Israel takes these events seriously and treats them as unique and remarkable. The memories proved real. The hopes evoked by the Mishnah's promise of sanctification of a world in static perfection did not prove real, for they had to compete with the grief of an entire century of mourning.

The most important change is the shift in historical thinking adumbrated in the pages of the Talmud of the Land of Israel, a shift from focus upon the Temple and its supernatural history to close attention to the people Israel and its natural, this-worldly history. Once Israel, holy Israel, had come to form the counterpart to the Temple and its supernatural life, that other history—Israel's—would stand at the center of things. Consequently a new sort of memorable event came to the fore in the Talmud of the Land of Israel: *it was the story of Israel's suffering, remembrance of that suffering on the one side, and an effort to explain events of such tragedy on the other.* So a composite "history" constructed out of the Yerushalmi's units of discourse which were pertinent to consequential events would contain long chapters on what happened to Israel, the Jewish people, and not only or mainly what had earlier occurred in the Temple.

The components of the historical theory of Israel's sufferings were manifold. First and foremost, history taught moral lessons. Historical events entered into the construction of a teleology for the Yerushalmi's system of Judaism as a whole. What the law demanded reflected the consequences of wrongful action on the part of Israel. So again Israel's own deeds defined the events of history. Rome's role, like Assyria's and Babylonia's, depended upon Israel's provoking divine wrath as it was executed by the great empire. This mode of thought comes to simple expression in what follows.

Y. Erubin 3:9

[IV B] R. Ba, R. Hiyya in the name of R. Yohanan: "'*Do not gaze at me because I am swarthy, because the sun has scorched me. My mother's sons were angry with me, they made me keeper of the vineyards; but, my own vineyard, I have not kept!*' [Song of Sol. 1:6]. What made me guard the vineyards? It is because of not keeping my own vineyard.

[C] "What made me keep two festival days in Syria? It is because I did not keep the proper festival day in the Holy Land.

[D] "I imagined that I would receive a reward for the two days, but I received a reward only for one of them.

[E] "Who made it necessary that I should have to separate two pieces of dough-offering from grain grown in Syria? It is because I did not separate a single piece of dough-offering in the Land of Israel."

Israel had to learn the lesson of its history in order to take command of its own destiny.

But this notion of determining one's own destiny should not be misunderstood. The framers of the Talmud of the Land of Israel were not telling the Jews to please God by doing commandments in order that they should thereby gain control of their own destiny. To the contrary, the paradox of the Yerushalmi's system lies in the fact that Israel can free itself of control by other nations *only* by humbly agreeing to accept God's rule. The nations—Rome, in the present instance—rest on one side of the balance while God rests on the other. Israel must then choose between them. There is no such thing for Israel as freedom from both God and the nations, total autonomy and independence. There is only a choice of masters, a ruler on earth or a ruler in heaven.

The framers of the Mishnah would certainly have concurred with propositions such as these. The fundamental affirmations of the Mishnah about the centrality of Israel's perfection in stasis—sanctification—readily prove congruent to the attitudes at hand. Once the Messiah's coming had become dependent upon Israel's condition and not upon Israel's actions in historical time, then the Mishnah's system will have imposed *its* fundamental and definitive character upon the Messiah myth. An eschatological teleology framed through that myth then would prove wholly appropriate to the method of the larger system of the Mishnah. When this fact has been fully appreciated we shall then have grasped the distinctive history of the myth of the Messiah in the formative history of Judaism.

What, after all, makes a messiah a false messiah? In this Talmud it is not his claim to save Israel, but his claim to save Israel without God's help. The meaning of the true Messiah is Israel's total submission, through the Messiah's gentle rule, to God's yoke and service. So God is not to be manipulated through Israel's humoring of heaven in rite and cult. The idea of keeping the commandments so as to please heaven and get God to do what Israel wants is totally incongruent to the text at hand. Keeping the commandments as a mark of humility before God is the rabbinic system of salvation. So Israel does not "save itself." Israel never controls its own destiny, either on earth or in heaven. The only choice is whether to cast one's fate into the hands of cruel, deceitful men or to trust in the living God of mercy and love. We shall now see how this critical position is embodied in the setting of discourse about the Messiah in the Talmud of the Land of Israel.

Bar Kokba above all exemplifies arrogance against God. He lost the war because of that arrogance. In particular, he ignored the authority of sages:

Y. Taanit 4:5

[X J] Said R. Yohanan, "Upon orders of Caesar Hadrian, they killed eight hundred thousand in Betar."

[K] Said R. Yohanan, "There were eighty thousand pairs of trumpeteers surrounding Betar. Each one was in charge of a number of troops. Ben Kozeba was there and he had two hundred thousand troops who, as a sign of loyalty, had cut off their little fingers.

[L] "Sages sent word to him, 'How long are you going to turn Israel into a maimed people?'

[M] "He said to them, 'How otherwise is it possible to test them?'

[N] "They replied to him, 'Whoever cannot uproot a cedar of Lebanon while riding on his horse will not be inscribed on your military rolls.'

[O] "So there were two hundred thousand who qualified in one way, and another two hundred thousand who qualified in another way."

[P] When he would go forth to battle, he would say, "Lord of the world! Do not help and do not hinder us! *'Hast thou not rejected us, O God? Thou dost not go forth, O God, with our armies'*" [Ps. 60:10].

[Q] Three and a half years did Hadrian besiege Betar.

[R] R. Eleazar of Modiin would sit on sackcloth and ashes and pray every day, saying "Lord of the ages! Do not judge in accord with strict judgment this day! Do not judge in accord with strict judgment this day!"

[S] Hadrian wanted to go to him. A Samaritan said to him, "Do not go to him until I see what he is doing, and so hand over the city [of Betar] to you. [Make peace . . . for you.]"

[T] He got into the city through a drain pipe. He went and found R. Eleazar of Modiin standing and praying. He pretended to whisper something in his ear.

[U] The townspeople saw [the Samaritan] do this and brought him to Ben Kozeba. They told him, "We saw this man having dealings with your friend."

[V] [Bar Kokba] said to him, "What did you say to him, and what did he say to you?"

[W] He [the Samaritan] said to him, "If I tell you, then the king will kill me, and if I do not tell you, then you will kill me. It is better that the king kill me, and not you.

[X] "[Eleazar] said to me, 'I should hand over my city.' ['I shall make peace. . . .']"

[Y] He turned to R. Eleazar of Modiin. He said to him, "What did this Samaritan say to you?"

[Z] He replied, "Nothing."

[AA] He said to him, "What did you say to him?"

[BB] He said to him, "Nothing."

[CC] [Ben Kozeba] gave [Eleazar] one good kick and killed him.

[DD] Forthwith an echo came forth and proclaimed the following verse:

[EE] "*Woe to my worthless shepherd, who deserts the flock! May the sword smite his arm and his right eye! Let his arm be wholly withered, his right eye utterly blinded!* [Zech. 11:17].

[FF] "You have murdered R. Eleazar of Modiin, the right arm of all Israel, and their right eye. Therefore may the right arm of that man wither, may his right eye be utterly blinded!"

[GG] Forthwith Betar was taken, and Ben Kozeba was killed.

We notice two complementary themes. First, Bar Kokba treats heaven with arrogance, asking God merely to keep out of the way. Second, he treats an especially revered sage with a parallel arrogance. The sage had the power to preserve Israel. Bar Kokba destroyed Israel's one protection. The result was inevitable.

The Messiah, the centerpiece of salvation history and hero of the tale, emerged as a critical figure. The historical theory of this Yerushalmi passage is stated very simply. In their view Israel had to choose between wars, either the war fought by Bar Kokba or the "war for Torah." "Why had they been punished? It was because of the weight of the war, for they had not wanted to engage in the struggles over the meaning of the Torah" (*Y. Ta.* 3:9 XVI I). Those struggles, which were ritual arguments about ritual matters, promised the only victory worth winning. Then Israel's history would be written in terms of wars over the meaning of the Torah and the decision of the law.

True, the skins are new but the wine is very old. For while we speak of the sages and learning, the message is familiar. It is Israel's history that works out and expresses Israel's relationship with God. The critical dimension of Israel's life, therefore, is salvation, the definitive trait a movement in time from now to then. It follows that the paramount and organizing category is history and its lessons. In the Yerushalmi we witness among the Mishnah's heirs a striking reversion to biblical convictions about the centrality of history in the definition of Israel's reality. The heavy weight of prophecy, apocalyptic, and biblical historiography, with their emphasis upon salvation and history as the indicator of Israel's salvation, stood against the Mishnah's quite separate thesis of what truly mattered. What from their viewpoint demanded description and required interpretation? It was the category of sanctification, for eternity. The true issue framed by history and apocalypse was how to move toward the foreordained end of salvation, how to act *in time* to reach salvation *at the end of time.* The Mishnah's capacity to posit an eschatology without a place for a historical Messiah takes a position beyond that of the entire antecedent sacred literature of Israel. Only one strand, the Priestly one, had ever taken so extreme a position on the centrality of sanctification and the peripheral nature of salvation. Wisdom had stood in between with its own concerns, drawing attention both to what happened and to what endured. But to Wisdom what finally mattered was not nature or supernature, but rather abiding relationships in historical time.

The Talmud of Babylonia, at the end, carried forward the innovations we have seen in the Talmud of the Land of Israel. In the view expressed here the principal result of Israel's loyal adherence to the Torah and its religious duties will be Israel's humble acceptance of God's rule. The humility makes God love Israel.

B. Hullin 89a

"*It was not because you were greater than any people that the Lord set his love upon you and chose you*" [Deut. 7:7]. The Holy One, blessed be he, said to Israel, "I love you because even when I bestow greatness upon you, you humble yourselves before me. I bestowed greatness upon Abraham, yet he said to me, '*I am but dust and ashes*' [Gen. 18:27]; upon Moses and Aaron, yet they said, '*But I am a worm and no man*' [Ps. 22:7]. But with the heathens it is not so. I bestowed greatness upon Nimrod, and he said, '*Come, let us build a city*' [Gen. 11:4]; upon Pharaoh, and he said, '*Who are they among all the gods of the counties?*' [2 Kings 18:35]; upon Nebuchadnezzar, and he said, '*I will ascend above the heights of the clouds*' [Isa. 14:14]; upon Hiram, king of Tyre, and he said, '*I sit in the seat of God, in the heart of the seas*' [Ezek. 28:2]."

So the system emerges complete, each of its parts stating precisely the same message as is revealed in the whole. The issue of the Messiah and the meaning of Israel's history framed through the Messiah myth convey in their terms precisely the same position that we find everywhere else in all other symbolic components of the rabbinic system and canon. The heart of the matter then is Israel's subservience to God's will as expressed in the Torah and embodied in the teachings and lives of the great sages. When Israel fully accepts God's rule, then the Messiah will come. Until Israel subjects itself to God's rule the Jews will be subjugated to pagan domination. Since the condition of Israel governs, Israel itself holds the key to its own redemption. But this it can achieve only by throwing away the key!

The paradox is evident: Israel acts to redeem itself through the opposite of self-determination, namely, by subjugating itself to God. Israel's power lies in its negation of power. Its destiny lies in giving up all pretense at deciding its own destiny. Thus weakness is the ultimate strength, forbearance the final act of self-assertion, passive resignation the sure step toward liberation. (The parallel is the crucified Christ.) Israel's freedom is engraved on the tablets of the commandments of God: to be free is freely to obey. That is not the meaning associated with these words in the minds of others who like the sages of the rabbinical canon declared their view of what Israel must do to secure the coming of the Messiah.

The passage praising Israel for its humility completes the circle begun with the description of Bar Kokba as arrogant and boastful. Gentile kings are boastful; Israelite kings are humble. So the Messiah myth deals with a very concrete and limited consideration of the national life and character. The theory of Israel's history and destiny as it was expressed within that myth interprets matters in terms of a single criterion. In context, the Messiah expresses the system's meaning and so makes it work.

The appearance of a messianic eschatology fully consonant with the larger characteristic of the rabbinic system—with its stress on the viewpoints and proof texts of Scripture, its interest in what was happening to Israel, its focus upon the national-historical dimension of the life of the group—indicates that the encompassing rabbinic system stands essentially autonomous of the prior mishnaic system. True, what had gone before was absorbed and fully assimilated, but the rabbinic system first appearing in the Talmud of the Land of Israel is different in the aggregate from the mishnaic system. It represents more, however, than a negative response to its predecessor. The rabbinic system of the two Talmuds took over the fundamental convictions of the Mishnaic worldview about the importance of Israel's constructing for itself a life beyond time. The rabbinic system then transformed the Messiah myth in its totality into an essentially ahistorical force. If people wanted to reach the end of time they had to rise above time, that is, history, and stand off at the side of great movements of political and military character. That is the message of the Messiah myth as it reaches full exposure in the rabbinic system of the two Talmuds. At its foundation it is *precisely* the message of teleology without eschatology expressed by the Mishnah and its associated documents. Accordingly, we cannot claim that the rabbinic or talmudic system in this regard constitutes a reaction against the mishnaic one. We must conclude, quite to the contrary, that in the Talmuds and their associated documents we see the restatement in classical-mythic form of the ontological convictions that had informed the minds of the second-century philosophers. The new medium contained the old and enduring message: Israel must turn away from time and change and submit to whatever happens so as to win for itself the only government worth having, that is, God's rule, accomplished through God's anointed agent the Messiah.

Epilogue
The Next Stage in the
Jewish-Christian Argument

I close with precisely the same conclusion that ended *Judaism in the Beginning of Christianity*. For I have no better insight to offer than the one with which I commenced these two corresponding books. The formative centuries of Christianity also tell us much about the development of Judaism as we know it. So formative Christianity demands to be studied in the context of formative Judaism, and formative Judaism in the context of formative Christianity. For throughout the history of the West these two religious traditions, along with Islam, have struggled in competition with one another. While in numbers the competing parties were scarcely equal, in theological and moral power each met its match in the other. What perpetually drew the one into competition with the other? Why could they not let one another be?

These questions draw attention in our own setting in modern times, after the Holocaust in particular, because at last the two great faiths of the West join together to confront a common challenge of renewal. So Judaism and Christianity work together in mutual respect as never before, in the service of one humanity in the image of one God. We are able to ask these questions because the spirit of our own age permits us to discuss them irenically, in ways utterly without precedent in the centuries before our own tragic times.

Both Judaism and Christianity claim to be the heirs and products of the Hebrew Scriptures—Tanakh to the Jews, Old Testament to the

Christians. Yet both great religious traditions derive indirectly from
the authority of those Scriptures as that authority has been mediated
through other holy books. The New Testament is the prism through
which the light of the Old comes to Christianity. The canon of rabbinical writings is the star that guides Jews to the revelation of Sinai,
the Torah. The claim of these two great religious traditions in all their
rich variety is for the veracity not merely of Scriptures, but also of
Scriptures as interpreted by the New Testament or the Talmud and
associated rabbinical writings.

The Hebrew Scriptures produced the two interrelated yet quite separate groups of religious societies that formed Judaism and Christianity. Developed along lines established during late antiquity, these
societies in modern times come near to each other in the West. Here
they live not merely side by side but together. However, while most
people are familiar with the story of the development of Christianity,
few are fully aware that Judaism constitutes a separate and distinctive
religious tradition. The differences are not limited to negations of
Christian beliefs—"Jews do not believe in this or that"—but also
extend to profound affirmations of Judaic ones. To understand the
Judaic dissent, one must comprehend the Judaic affirmation in its own
terms.

What is it that historical Judaism sought to build? What are its
primary emphases, its evocative symbols? What lies at the heart of
the human situation as constructed and imagined by classical Judaism?
The answers come first of all from the pages of the rabbinic canon
and related literature. From late antiquity onward the rabbis of the
Torah, written and oral, supplied the proof texts, constructed the society, shaped the values, occupied the mind, and formed the soul of
Judaism. For all the human concerns brought by Christians to the
figure of Christ, the Jews looked to Torah. While the Christ-event
stands at the beginning of the tradition of Christianity, the rabbinic
canon comes at the end of the formation of the Judaism contained in
it. It is the written record of the constitution of the life of Israel, the
Jewish people, long after the principles and guidelines of that constitution had been worked out and effected in everyday life. Moreover,
the early years of Christianity were dominated first by the figure of
the Master, then his disciples and their followers bringing the gospel

to the nations; the formative years of rabbinic Judaism saw a small group of men who were not dominated by a single leader but who effected an equally far-reaching revolution in the life of the Jewish nation.

Both the apostles and the rabbis thus reshaped the antecedent religion of Israel, and both claimed to be Israel. That pre-Christian, pre-rabbinic religion of Israel, for all its variety, exhibited common traits: belief in one God, reverence for and obedience to the revelation contained in the Hebrew Scriptures, veneration of the Temple in Jerusalem (while it stood), and expectation of the coming of a Messiah to restore all the Jews to the land of Palestine and to bring to a close the anguish of history. The Christian Jews concentrated on the last point, proclaiming that the Messiah had come in Jesus; the rabbinic Jews focused on the second, teaching that only through the full realization of the imperatives of the Hebrew Scriptures, Torah, as interpreted and applied by the rabbis, would the people merit the coming of the Messiah. The rabbis, moreover, claimed alone to possess the whole Torah of Moses. This is central to their doctrine: Moses had revealed not only the message now written down in his books, but also an oral Torah which was formulated and transmitted to his successors and they to theirs through Joshua, the prophets, the sages, scribes, and other holy men, and finally to the rabbis of the day. For the Christian, therefore, the issue of the Messiah predominated; for the rabbinic Jew, the issue of Torah; and for both, the question of salvation was crucial.

What form would Western civilization have taken had the Judaic rather than the Christian formulation of the heritage of Hebrew Scriptures come to predominate? What sort of society would have emerged? How would people have regulated their affairs? What would have been the shape of the prevailing value systems? Behind the immense varieties of Christian life and Christian and post-Christian society stand the evocative teachings and theological and moral convictions assigned by Christian belief to the figure of Christ. To be a Christian in some measure meant and means to seek to be like him, in one of the many ways in which Christians envisaged him. To be a Jew may similarly be reduced to the single, pervasive symbol of Judaism: Torah. To be a Jew meant to live the life of Torah, in one of the many ways in which the masters of Torah taught.

We know what the figure of Christ has meant to the art, music, and literature of the West; the church to its politics, history, and piety; Christian faith to its values and ideals. It is much harder to say what Torah would have meant to creative arts, the course of relations among nations and people, the hopes and aspirations of ordinary folk. For between Christ, universally known and triumphant, and Torah, the spiritual treasure of a tiny, harassed, abused people, seldom fully known and never long victorious, stands the abyss: mastery of the world on the one side, the sacrifice of the world on the other. Perhaps the difference comes at the very start when the Christians, despite horrendous suffering, determined to conquer and save the world and to create the new Israel. The rabbis, unmolested and unimpeded, set forth to transform and regenerate the old Israel. For the former, the arena of salvation was all humankind, the actor was a single man. For the latter, the course of salvation began with Israel, God's first love, and the stage was that singular but paradigmatic society, the Jewish people.

To save the world the apostle had to suffer in and for it, appear before magistrates, subvert empires. To redeem the Jewish people the rabbi had to enter into, share, and reshape the life of the community, deliberately eschew the politics of nations and patiently submit to empires. The vision of the apostle extended to all nations and peoples. Immediate suffering therefore was the welcome penalty to be paid for eventual, universal dominion. The rabbi's eye looked upon Israel, and in his love for Jews he sought not to achieve domination or to risk martyrdom, but rather to labor for social and spiritual transformation which was to be accomplished through the complete union of his life with that of the community. The one was prophet to the nations, the other priest to the people. No wonder then that the apostle earned the crown of martyrdom but prevailed in history, while the rabbi received martyrdom when it came only as one of the people. He gave up the world and its conversion in favor of the people and their re-generation. In the end the people hoped that through their regener-ation, if need be through their suffering, the world also would be redeemed. But the people would be the instrument and not the crafts-men of redemption, which God alone would bring.

The ancient rabbis looked out upon a world destroyed and still smoking in the aftermath of calamity, but they speak of rebirth and renewal. The holy Temple lay in ruins, but they ask about sanctification. The old history was over, but they look forward to future history. Theirs, as we see, is a message that what is true and real is the opposite of what people perceive. God stands for paradox. Strength comes through weakness, salvation through acceptance and obedience, sanctification through the ordinary and profane which can be made holy. Now to informed Christians the mode of thought must prove remarkably familiar. For the cross that stands for weakness yields salvation, and the crucified criminal is king and savior. That is the foolishness to which the apostle Paul makes reference. Yet the greater the "nonsense"—life out of the grave, eternity from death—the deeper the truth, the richer the paradox! So here we have these old Jews, one group speaking of sanctification of Israel the people, the other of salvation of Israel and the world. Separately they are thinking along the same lines, coming to conclusions remarkably congruent to one another, affirming the paradox of God in the world, of humanity in God's image in the rabbinical framework; of God in the flesh in the Christian. Is it not time for the joint heirs of ancient Israel's Scripture and hope to meet once more, in humility, before the living God? Along with all humanity, facing backward toward Auschwitz and total destruction, and forward toward complete annihilation of the world as we know it—is it not time?

The argument has ended. The age of building has begun.

Indexes

GENERAL INDEX

145

INDEX OF SCRIPTURE AND TRACTATES